# Madison's Alternatives: The Jeffersonian Republicans and the Coming of War, 1805—1812

Robert A. Rutland

**University of Virginia**

**The America's Alternatives Series**

Edited by **Harold M. Hyman**

# Madison's Alternatives:

The Jeffersonian
Republicans and the
Coming of War, 1805—1812

**J. B. Lippincott Company**
Philadelphia/New York/Toronto

Copyright © 1975, by J. B. Lippincott Company

This book is fully protected by copyright and, with the exception of brief excerpts for review, no part of it may be reproduced in any form by print, photoprint, microfilm, or by any other means without the written permission of the publishers.

ISBN-0-397-47331-1
Library of Congress Catalog Card Number 75-2088
Printed in the United States of America
1 3 5 7 9 8 6 4 2

Library of Congress Cataloging in Publication Data

Rutland, Robert Allen, 1922-
    Madison's alternatives.

    (The America's alternatives series)
    Bibliography: p.
    1. United States—Politics and government—1801-1815.
I. Title.
E338.R88        320.9'73'046        75-2088
ISBN 0-397-47331-1

# Contents ─────────────

# Foreword

"When you judge decisions, you have to judge them in the light of what there was available to do it," noted Secretary of State George C. Marshall to the Senate Committees on the Armed Services and Foreign Relations in May, 1951.[1] In this spirit, each volume in the "America's Alternatives" series examines the past for insights which History—perhaps only History—is peculiarly fitted to offer. In each volume the author seeks to learn why decision makers in crucial public policy or, more rarely, private choice situations adopted a course and rejected others. Within this context of choices, the author may ask what influence then-existing expert opinion, administrative structures, and budgetary factors exerted in shaping decisions? What weights did constitutions or traditions have? What did men hope for or fear? On what information did they base their decisions? Once a decision was made, how was the decision maker able to enforce it? What attitudes prevailed toward nationality, race, region, religion, or sex, and how did these attitudes modify results?

We freely ask such questions of the events of our time. This "America's Alternatives" volume transfers appropriate versions of such queries to the past.

In examining those elements that were a part of a crucial historical decision, the author has refrained    m making judgments based upon attitudes, information, or values that were not current at the time the decision was made. Instead, as much as possible, he or she has explored the past in terms of data and prejudices known to persons contemporary to the event.

[1] U.S. Congress, Senate, Hearings Before the Committees on the Armed Services and the Foreign Relations of the United States, *The Military Situation in the Far East,* 82d Cong., 2d sess., part I, p. 382. Professor Ernest R. May's "Alternatives" volume directed me to this source and quotation.

Nevertheless, the following reconstruction of one of America's major alternative choices speaks implicitly and frequently explicitly to present concerns.

In form, this volume consists of a narrative and analytical historical essay (Part One), within which the author has identified by use of headnotes (i.e., Alternative 1) the choices which he believes were actually before the decision makers with whom he is concerned.

Part Two of this volume contains, in whole or in part, the most appropriate source documents that illustrate the Part One Alternatives. The Part Two documents and Part One essay are keyed for convenient learning use (i.e., references in Part One will direct readers to appropriate Part Two documents). The volume's Part Three offers the user further guidance in the form of a Bibliographical Essay.

Looking backward to the origins of what Americans call the War of 1812 allows readers insights from that hindsight not available to Jeffersonian decision makers, including President James Madison. Few living scholars have studied Madison's letters and other writings as intently as Professor Robert A. Rutland, who is presently editor of the massive *Papers of James Madison* publication project at the University of Virginia. In the following pages, Professor Rutland offers a hard, lively review of what became a road to war, and an improved understanding of why that generation chose it.

Harold M. Hyman
Rice University

# Acknowledgments ═══════

Harold Hyman's deft skill in handling authors as well as documents must be recognized, along with the useful discussions concerning Madison's relationship with Jefferson carried on with my neighbor, Dumas Malone. Frank C. Mevers III helped clarify certain points through his useful compilation of the War of 1812 materials for the *Papers of James Madison*. Jeanne Sisson's speed and accuracy at the typewriter were indispensable. She not only met the deadline but saved me from several errors by her perceptive reading of the manuscript while she typed.

# Part One

## War and Peace and the Republican Ideal

# 1

# War and Peace and the Republican Ideal

Pacifists and historians have long cited Benjamin Franklin's neat aphorism—"There never was a good war or a bad peace"—as a summary view of the most evil of all human institutions. "Ez fer War, I call it murder," Hosea Biglow announced in James Russell Lowell's influential series of antiadministration articles in 1848. Between these two observations we perceive viewpoints appealing and seemingly universal: peace is worth any sacrifice, and war is the most heinous of crimes. Yet within a short time after Franklin spoke he was supporting a revolution, and Lowell's commentary soon was cited as a kind of backhanded endorsement for war, provided it was fought for a justifiable cause. Thus Americans from our earliest colonial days have tended to follow the lead of mankind throughout history by excoriating war on the one hand while holding a sword in the other. "Mr. Madison's war," as the sneering Federalists said in 1812, is a notable case in point.

James Madison deserves attention in any study of war not because he was either a military hero or a pacifist, but rather because Madison was probably the most intelligent man ever to occupy the White House; and yet in the views of many historians, public men, and political scientists Madison pursued disastrous policies that resulted in the War of 1812. If intellectual, rational James Madison could not avoid a war, what can be expected of lesser men in the same seat of power? In this study we are not concerned with whether the war itself was an enormous blunder, but whether Madison as secretary of state from 1801 to 1809, and then as president, pursued policies and chose from alternative courses of action a route which ultimately brought on a declaration of war. The record cannot be rewritten—the War of 1812 was fought, and historians still may argue as to whether it was won or lost—but our concern is whether Madison carried out his responsibilities as a professed lover of peace, as a believer in reason over raw power, and as the chief magistrate of a republic.

## Madison's Concept of War and Changing Realities

At the outset, we can assume that Madison's natural disposition was toward peace. Throughout much of his life he sought to avoid confrontation whenever possible (see Document 1). Political campaigns were as abhorrent to him as military ones; he learned his first lesson in practical politics when he was defeated in a state legislative race owing to his disdain for rough-and-tumble politics. Thereafter, Madison realized that whether one battled for votes in Orange County, Virginia, or for neutral rights on the high seas, there were certain methods of conduct that had to be observed. However, standing for office or sailing into a naval battle had one thing in common: risk. What Madison consistently tried to avoid was a high degree of risk in his personal life and in his conduct of national affairs. If there is any tragic aspect of his long career as a public servant, it is the fact that on the scales of history his services in 1787 are weighed against his apparent failure in 1812. When the United States went to war against England, the American who shouldered the whole burden of blame had to be the president whose hands had guided foreign affairs for the preceding eleven years.

The documents chosen to illustrate the pathway toward war are selected to give readers some insight into Madison as an ardent republic theoretician cast in the role of a policy maker. After Jefferson became president in 1801, all the circumstances seemed to point toward a salutary tenure for Madison as secretary of state. The Peace of Amiens had been only recently concluded, thus ending (or so it seemed) a long Franco-British war that had disrupted international relations and had involved the United States in a quasi war with its onetime French ally. In the breathing spell allowed by this peace, Jefferson and Madison strove to create through "the Republican Ascendancy" a political system that would undergird the Constitution, assure prosperity in the land, and provide an example to the world of what free men could accomplish.*

The Jeffersonian program of 1801 now seems a distant memory far removed from the realities of the twentieth century, although the ideal of an agrarian republic still retains appeal for many Americans. Both Jefferson and Madison had been participants in a revolution which touched a spark in Europe, and in the interval between 1776 and 1801 a new generation came along to carry forward the torch meant to proclaim life, liberty, equality, fraternity, and the pursuit of happiness. In the hands of Napoleon, however, that torch became the firebrand of war. The presence of Napoleon disrupted any peaceful progression toward the betterment of mankind and loosened a nationalistic drive that released those atavistic qualities present in even the most enlightened men. As von Clausewitz noted, whatever tendency nations exhibited toward a rational and peaceable conduct of their international relations came crashing down in the wake of Napoleon's ambition. To Jefferson and Madison, war was to some degree an extension of diplomatic maneuvering—a contest (even when on a global scale) of movements and negotiations. The emerging Napoleonic concept of total war was foreign to their thinking. While these gentlemanly Virginians were still mentally enmeshed in the kinds of warfare that developed in early centuries, they were

*The Republicans of 1800-1827 were not the precursors of the modern Republican party. Liberal Republicans changed their party's name to "Democratic" in 1828.

not able to comprehend fully the Napoleonic policy or the British reaction to that policy.

Any approach to an understanding of the policies of Jefferson and Madison from 1803, when England and France renewed their conflict, must consider this gap between the new realities and the perceptions of the American presidents who sought avenues of escape from a war with either France or England or both. Although the technology of war was still old-fashioned in 1805, the acceleration of historical processes induced by the French Revolution had led to the use of mass armies, with crushing battles fought to destroy completely the enemy army so that the vanquished party had no negotiating room left. For Napoleon, war was no chess game played by conventional rules, but rather a life-and-death struggle which, if successfully carried on by every available means, would leave the enemy absolutely powerless.

The British came to understand this, and in time their statesmen believed that all that stood between civilization as men knew it and a new form of barbarism was the British navy. It is not an exaggeration to say that this fear of Napoleon reached down to the alleys of London, and even little children as they hopscotched along the cobblestones recited a chant about the boogie-man "Boney! Boney!" Napoleon was a menace to the British in 1803 as Hitler was to the Europeans in 1940—dreadfully evil and bent upon becoming their master. But Jefferson and Madison did not see this. To be sure, the Americans realized that Napoleon was a counterrevolutionary and did not trust him, but they did not take into account the implications of warfare that embraced not only ships and guns as weapons but also trade policies, propaganda techniques, and even human starvation as part of an arsenal. "Our wish ought to be that he who has armies may not have Dominion of the sea, and that he who has Dominion of the sea may be one who has no armies," Jefferson ventured in 1806, when the spectacle of a devastating European war was clearly apparent.[1]

Indeed, there was something in Jefferson and Madison that made them old-fashioned men still dreaming that Hobbes was wrong and Locke was right, that enlightened men could see the folly of war and long for the bliss promised by the biblical setting of one's own vine and fig tree. The business of mankind, to these American statesmen, was to extend the fruits of science and industry to all deserving citizens. Neither Jefferson nor Madison could comprehend a man or a nation which gave the highest priority to pomp, glory, and military power. To some degree, Americans since their day have suffered from the same naiveté. "Democracy has stimulated the will of the people to eliminate war, although it has not yet enlightened their intelligence as to the means," as Quincy Wright observed.[2] Accordingly, every instance in the American experience which has brought either wars or threats of wars has also brought protesting groups which a Napoleon or a Hitler would not tolerate. Testimony for this democratic outcry against war is manifest from 1812 down to the Kent State massacre in 1970.

When the expectations of peace are unusually high, the realities of a postwar situation are the more devastating, as occurred after World War I with all its slogan-promises for peace and political justice. In the backlash of bitterness stemming from the disillusionment of the 1920s, Americans were then willing to accept the idea that war was an instrument of brute force, and the public assumed that what was being said in editorials and on soapboxes was true: all wars were concocted by arrogant generals allied with greedy munitions makers. Fifty years later, Americans may still have misconceptions about war. All wars are not bad, nor are all peaceful eras good, despite Franklin's charming aphorism. At least Jefferson and Madison assumed that our War for Independence had created more good than evil, and we can assume that without World War II the reign of terror over law might still have powerful advocates.

The War of 1812 is a struggle with its comic-tragic aspects, but until fairly recent times there was much assumed, and little known, about the origins of this conflict. Superpatriots who declared that the United States "never lost a war, or won a peace," had not studied the intricate story of how the country walked into a diplomatic maze and finally chopped its way out in cumbersome fashion. One president lost his reputation (with later historians), another president survived the negotiating, and a third president-to-be made his reputation in the great battle fought after the peace treaty was signed. Reputations were trampled and vaulted, but something tangible came out of the War of 1812—nationhood. With Napoleon finally defeated and England ready to exert pressure at the Congress in Vienna, the United States established itself as no mere feisty former colonial dependency. The growing country had vast unsettled areas, seemingly unlimited natural resources, and a definite national pride borne out of the ability to take on the world's greatest power—twice—and win at least once and hold on for a tie in the second go-round. Europeans, bewildered and decimated by wars they were losing at great cost, could admire (or at least comprehend) the significance of such a war. As Europe smoldered and wept for her dead, the two powers still on their feet and slugging were members of the same family—both English-speaking and holding on to the same fables beyond Magna Carta. Somehow the vindictiveness and revenge so common to struggles on the Continent would not prevail in such circumstances, although at the time—if the newspaper essayists had been credible—a rapprochement between the lion and eagle was unthinkable. Yet the Monroe Doctrine, a mere decade away, was one of the first manifestations of this newfound respect for the United States.

## The Background of the War

Here we are concerned not with the aftermath of the War of 1812, however, but rather with the steps that preceded the final diplomatic breach and led to combat. The deepest roots of the conflict lay back in the 1780s, when unsettled terms of the Treaty of Paris had led to all sorts of claims and counterclaims of violations by both parties. The grievances in the American

West were of Indians coddled by the British and hostile to frontiersmen; while in the East the Yankee ship captains stood in anger when a British boarding party occasionally swooped down and spirited off good sturdy seamen on flimsy evidence. Merchants in nearly every seaport remembered the old lucrative trade with the British West Indies that had previously brought such huge profits, but which was now restricted. These conditions grew out of the War for Independence and were bad enough in themselves, but once Napoleon challenged the British all the old complaints took on extra dimensions as British men-of-war commenced a blockade in 1804 that denied the basic American position in maritime commerce: free ships make free goods. The labyrinth of international law would be searched with painstaking regularity in the hope that British leaders would accept a principle that logic declared they could not, that is, to allow neutral powers to supply their enemies with food and goods.

James Madison was a logical man, a hard-working secretary of state (see Documents 1 and 2), and he would be an indefatigable president. There has been a tendency to portray Madison as the bright young man who somehow faded as his responsibility grew. Even so late as 1970, a Madison biographer could write: "But the President, whom the celebrants of 1815 praised for his contribution to ending the war, was to receive little commendation from posterity. Indeed, not only did Madison fail to win lasting esteem from the Treaty of Ghent, he came to be thought of as the worst of the wartime presidents between John Adams and Harry Truman. That he took the country into a war that it was unprepared to fight and mismanaged it from the time it began came to be the simple and prevailing view."[3] A popular historian in 1972 saw Madison much as his Federalist opponents had viewed him, after the war began; a commander-in-chief with huge horse pistols strapped to his waist, "looking less like the nation's Commander-in-Chief than a small child dressed up to play war."[4] Could it be that the Federalists' attitude toward Madison had, in the long run, prevailed to the extent that a negative judgment was handed to posterity?

Perhaps Madison does deserve better treatment, but the point of this series is to give the reader a clean slate and allow him to make his own judgment. The documents printed here have been chosen with a determination to build no case either for or against Madison, or in a broader sense, the Jefferson-Madison concept of republican foreign relations. The reader should constantly be aware of the republican mentality as exemplified by both Jefferson and Madison, for in justice to their program they must be taken on their own ground—not on ours. Isolated from the scenes of European war, the American of 1805 or 1812—the Kentuckian or the upstate New Yorker—had no true picture of what the new warfare involved. To him, as to his president, war was a limited military action of short duration and almost certain victory. Viewed in that light, war held no great fear, and in some ways was highly justifiable to a people frequently accustomed to seeing blood in street fights (with eye-gouging possible), and who viewed farm and road accidents as a commonplace. In fact, the frontier conditions and the migration from Europe had bred into the American character a unique willingness to take risks, along with a confidence that the result would be favorable. A certain recklessness, then, was a fact of life in Madison's young nation. This too must be taken into account by readers in the twentieth century, when a re-creation of the earlier mental attitude is necessary if we are to understand the thought processes at work in Washington between 1805 and 1812.

Another factor that must be considered is that wars resulting from a sudden *cause célèbre* have a drama that is not found in wars which come after a breakdown in long negotiations. The one involves surprise, indignation, anger, and great passion; while wars coming at the end of fruitless diplomatic maneuvers appear to be the result of a cumbersome process probably guided by inept managers. The attack on Pearl Harbor left no alternatives, but the calculated efforts of Madison to steer a neutral America clear of the icebergs in British and French diplomatic waters do not excite sympathy in the casual observer. As a matter of fact, a similar kind of diplomatic deterioration did not occur in American history until 1917, so that in the perspective of history the War of 1812 has none of that saving grace bestowed on conflicts which have resulted from real (or imagined) but immediate provocation.[5] In the final failure of the diplomacy of the Madison administration, the provocations counted for little as compared to the national insult implied in the British Orders in Council. The reader should bear this in mind throughout his examination of the documents, for the judgment of most historians has finally rested on the proposition that nothing contributed so much to the final rupture with England as those detested decrees that seemed to make the United States a minion of the British empire. In his war message to Congress (see Document 15), Madison covered all the indignities heaped on Americans since 1803, but foremost among the grievances had to be "the sweeping system of Blockades, under the name of orders in council; which has been moulded and managed as might best suit its political views, its commercial jealousies, or the avidity of British cruisers." The Orders in Council amounted to nothing less than a war on American commerce (see Document 5-b). By Madison's final chain of logic, there was nothing left to do but fight.

## Notes

1. Dumas Malone, *Jefferson the President, Second Term, 1805-1809* (Boston: Little, Brown & Co., 1974), p. 95.

2. Quincy Wright, *A Study of War*, 2 vols. (Chicago: University of Chicago Press, 1965), vol. 1, p. 5.

3. Harold S. Schultz, *James Madison*, Rulers and Statesmen of the World Series (New York: Twayne Co., 1970), p. 187.

4. Walter Lord, *The Dawn's Early Light* (New York: Norton, 1972), p. 107.

5. To be explicit—the British march to Lexington-Concord to confiscate militia stores, the reaction of Santa Ana to an American border incident, the firing on Fort Sumter, the *Maine* sinking, Pearl Harbor, the crossing of the 38th parallel in Korea, and the Gulf of Tonkin incident. But, on the other hand, the list of such events which did not result in a declared war is beyond calculation—such as the captures of *L'Insurgente*, the *Chesapeake* affair, the *Alabama* seizure, the *Panay* sinking, and the U-2 incident over the USSR.

# 2

# The State of American Sovereignty

When Jefferson, Madison, Gallatin, and others in the inner Republican circle pushed aside the Federalist program in 1801 they intended to turn the direction of the nation toward republican ideals (*Alternative 1:* see Document 1). With Madison at his side, Jefferson had only disdain for both the ceremony of his predecessor and the pretentiousness of the small diplomatic corps in the new capital. Their Virginia-bred republicanism, in practical terms, was a commitment to encourage the exporting of American farm products while reducing the national debt through the customs collected on foreign imports. They believed in frugality in government, and except for the White House wine list their tastes were as republican as their dress. Jefferson's casual first reception of the British minister while wearing an old dressing gown and house slippers was not meant to be an affront to the king's representative, but the diplomat chose to make it so, and in their lighter moments Madison and Jefferson may have looked back on Mr. Merry's indignation with amusement.

Little else that happened in Anglo-American relations left room for smiles, however, for the uneasy Peace of Amiens was shattered in 1803, and from that time on the diplomatic problems of the United States grew apace. Jefferson and Madison had long since shaken off their infatuation with the French as they realized that Napoleon was a confirmed autocrat whose very being was a denial of republicanism. Yet the opportunity Napoleon presented—the purchase of Louisiana—came almost as a shock. Thus the two Virginians found themselves on a crest of popularity once the great "empire for liberty" had been delivered into their hands by the French emperor's surprising role as an imperial land agent. Once Louisiana had been acquired, only Canada and the Floridas remained outside the American political and geographic orbit. The expansionism that seemed inevitable to men living within earshot of the Niagara Falls or the Chattahoochee River was against the grain of republican philosophy, but the problems of dealing with England, France, and Spain made the difficulty with frontiersmen hold a low priority.

## James Madison as Diplomat and Statesman

Probably no American secretary of state was ever so well-versed in international law as Madison, nor as hard-working. Still, the element of luck appeared to count for more in American dealings with foreign powers than Madison's skill as a negotiator. Although the modern historian Irving Brant has done much repair work on Madison's reputation, it is likely that Henry Adams's generally harsh judgment on Madison created a distorted portrait that still is fixed in the public mind. For example, in one volume of his monumental multivolume history of the Jefferson and Madison administration, Adams translated a French diplomat's note written early in 1806 which drew a most unflattering portrait of Madison, the cabinet member. Brant took the original manuscript some 146 years later and had a second translation made, concluding that a grave injustice had been done to Madison.

> The picture of Madison as a half-fainting, shifty-eyed weakling comes entirely from Adams, not from Turreau. There is no reason to suppose that the historian intentionally falsified this document, but that does not alter the effect. The blunders in translation, made in gloating innocence . . . have probably done more to blast Madison's posthumous reputation than all the misrepresentations of his Federalist adversaries.[1]

In his effort to defend Madison, Brant doubtless leaned in the other direction. Madison may not have been—indeed probably was unjustly accused of being—a man of physical unattractiveness; but when Adams criticized Madison's political trimming or his tendency toward prolixity, he was treading on firm ground. "Madison's opinions on this subject, as on some others, were elusive," Adams wrote of the Florida question, "perhaps no clearer to himself than to readers of his writings."[2] But Adams, for all his prejudices, could also perceive Madison's strength as a thinker who, when under fire, could calmly analyze a situation. "His faults of style and vagueness of thought almost wholly disappeared in the heat of controversy; his defence was cool, his attack keen, as though his sixty years weighed lightly the day when he first got his young antagonist at his mercy."[3]

Since the definitive biography of Madison has yet to appear, we must look to the documents for confirmation or denial of a viewpoint somewhere between Adams and Brant. "James Madison had a brilliant flair for diplomacy," Brant insisted in an early volume, and he never retreated from this assessment.[4] Where Brant saw Madison's shortcomings as human failings dictated more by sensitivity than as real weakness, Adams found Madison a dangerous "enemy" in domestic political battles but a naive and essentially inept cabinet officer and president.[5]

Whatever Madison's shortcomings, few historians have been as blunt as Adams in their assessment of Madison's public services. Probably the most influential textbook in the field of United States history in the twentieth century has been the venerable work, *The Growth of the American Republic*, by Samuel Eliot Morison and Henry S. Commager. This widely used book certainly has helped perpetuate the Adams-drawn stereotype. The authors gave Madison some credit for cleverness but called him "unimpressive in personality . . . [and] unable to inspire loyalty in his subordinates, or enthusiasm in the nation."[6] They also regarded Madison's cabinet choices as mediocrities, excepting Gallatin, which was a judgment hardly to be questioned. Bradford Perkins has been more kind to Madison in describing him as "no mere sycophant" but rather as "a tremendous worker" who became a principal architect of American foreign policy during sixteen crucial years. Still, Perkins indicated that when compared to Jefferson, "Madison's mind ran in narrower channels ... he was less decisive, tending always to magnify the dangers of any proposed course."[7] Ralph Ketcham's biography (1971) of Madison is somewhat apologetic for his subject's Washington years, as his section on the cabinet of 1809 indicated. "Political necessity and sectional balance seemed to force mediocrity on Madison," a sympathetic Ketcham concluded.[8]

## Conflicts in Economic Plans and Priorities

Let the reader reflect upon these interpretations as he fashions his own opinion of Madison as a national leader and international statesman. The question must be asked whether Madison was a firm decision maker who chose from several alternatives, or whether the rush of history engulfed him. Since Madison and Jefferson were so attuned to each other's viewpoints and so much in agreement, their rare relationship almost dictated that Madison would (in the presidency) be no innovator but rather a committed Jeffersonian Republican (*Alternative 1*: see Document 3). That meant, in turn, that Madison would have to work along the lines which he and Jefferson had pursued from 1806 onward—firm in their belief that ultimately economic coercion would accomplish the same kind of miracle that had been wrought in 1765-1766 when the Stamp Act had been repealed (*Alternative 2*: see Document 5). In their minds, the issue was not whether war should result but whether forbearance and denial would not make actual war a paltry substitute for embargoes and pressures from the mercantile community in London. As planters with memories stretching back to colonial times, they both respected the power of the London merchants, and it was difficult for Madison and Jefferson or other southern planters to discern any substantive difference between the colonial associations of the 1760s and 1770s and the economic stresses inherent in an embargo policy.

Perhaps there was a basic fallacy in the Madison-Jefferson program which they were loath to admit. Any economic coercion is more likely to succeed if the recalcitrant party which is stopping trade with one nation can quickly shift to another market. If American storekeepers wanted to sell British steel hatchets instead of French ones, it was good business to send American wheat to London as payment for those hatchets. But if no wheat went to England, and no English hatchets came back in repayment, and hatchets were vital, then either British hatchets would be smuggled in or inferior French ones would be bought at a higher price. If there is anything the American merchant has always been, it has been practical, and practicality produced profits for Americans that made them rivals to their British cousins who greatly resented all controls.

Madison failed to appreciate the zeal merchants would display when the ultimate question was profits or patriotism. As a southern planter, Madison shared with Jefferson a certain detachment about the world of business that made him unable to understand the world of the countinghouse. Since he was never bothered by any conflict over the priorities of his allegiance to the Union—first, last, and always—Madison never could comprehend how some citizens of the United States consistently acted as though their first duty was to fill their purses. This is a conflict of long standing, of course, but in Madison's case the difficulty led to some enormous misconceptions. In time it seemed that most of New England was going in one direction and the rest of the country headed in another, for after the Embargo Act of 1807 there was a definite schism in the nation that had at its root a pursuit of profits. Accordingly, even before Madison became president, he had to go to the negotiating table hampered by the knowledge that the New England Federalists were out to wreck the Republican answer to Anglo-French coercion. "With all their firmness and independence, and their high-toned integrity and sense of honor, probably no class of men in our country, no partisans, were ever more prejudiced and bigotted in their political sympathies, or more bitter and vindictive in their enmities, than the federalists of 1812," John Quincy Adams recalled.[9] Adams knew whereof he spoke, and in our consideration of Madison's dilemma we must take into account the disaffection manifested in maritime New England years before he became president.

The fact that the commercial centers of the North were dominated by Federalists had been a discordant note for the Republican administration of Jefferson, and the lack of harmony heightened despite Madison's hopes for national unity. Long distrustful of western migrations, the New Englanders saw the Louisiana Purchase as another means of depopulating the original Union while transferring the fulcrum of political power westward. Renewal of the Anglo-French war placed a new kind of pressure on Jefferson and his secretary of state, for the first two presidents had only been troubled by one bellicose party, whereas the Republicans were faced with two powers clutching at each other's throats. Coming at a time when the American merchant marine was rising rapidly in international trade, the blockades (either real or on paper) threatened to strangle American commerce just as the world demand for cotton, sugar, coffee, lumber, and other commodities was becoming attuned to the demands of the new industrialism. In May, 1806, England declared a blockade of all French-held ports from Brest to the Elbe, with a warning that neutral ships that attempted to reach French-controlled harbors would be seized and confiscated. Impressments of American seamen by British boarding parties had been a festering grievance for years, but now the British sent their ships hovering off the American coast, to intercept ships bound for France, and to seize alleged deserters from the British navy. "This act of aggression on our commerce," John Quincy Adams observed, "for such was its effect and such was its design, was the main moving cause of the war of 1812."[10]

## Threats to American Commerce and Sovereignty

Most Americans agreed that impressment was a great evil, and were equally infuriated by the menacing British fleet in American waters that preyed on American vessels. In 1805 a popular pamphlet in England, *War in Disguise, or the Frauds of a Neutral Flag*, was widely acclaimed for its attack on American neutrality and its implication that the United States was becoming a formidable rival to the British maritime fleet. Madison, a student of international law for most of his life, also entered the pamphleteer ranks early in 1806, at about the time *War in Disguise* was reaching America. Madison's anonymous work, *Examination of the British Doctrine, which subjects to capture a Neutral Trade* . . . , was so long and tedious in its arguments that even Brant confesses the work suffered from "massive unreadability" (see Documents 3-a and 3-b). Madison was attacking the so-called Rule of 1756—a British edict worked out during the Seven Years War, and reimposed by the *Essex* decision in May, 1805, to prevent neutral ships from carrying goods in wartime that they could not legally have brought to port in peace. Madison argued that the British had invoked the rule when it suited their convenience, and relaxed it for the same reason. More important, the British Rule of 1756 was a violation of international law—"its *true foundation a mere superiority of force*." No lawyer could have summed up the situation better than layman Madison, who wanted to believe that law was superior to firepower. Madison demonstrated the absurdity of a British policy which justified the capture of American ships carrying French colonial products while "she trades herself with her enemies, and invites them to trade with her colonies." While Madison thus charged England with duplicity and unlawful acts on the high seas, his critics in New England prayed for an English triumph over Napoleon and weakened whatever force the secretary of state's argument had. "The wind of the cannon ball that smashes John Bull's brains out, will lay us on our backs with all our tired honours in the dirt," Federalist Fisher Ames canted.[11]

Amidst this love-hate relationship, the president himself had some second thoughts about England. For a time Jefferson considered the possibility of an Anglo-American alliance to ward off the Napoleonic menace.[12] As this was a faint hope at best, Jefferson abandoned the thought of a rapprochement with England and used some of the language of Madison's pamphlet in his annual message in December, 1805. After reviewing the depredations on American commerce by the belligerents, Jefferson recommended a modest gunboat-building program, a reorganization of the militia, and a ban on the export of munitions.

For some Americans this was answering a cannon-blast with a slingshot, and not a few blamed Madison for the failure to mobilize the country with tougher policies. "The President wants nerve—he has not even confidence in himself," Kentucky Senator John Adair complained. "For more than a year he has been in the habit of trusting almost implicitly in Mr. Madison. Madison has acquired a complete ascendancy over him."[13] Jefferson's second term had barely started before his critics bayed at his heels either for not taking a more determined line with the British or for not slamming the door on France. With the Florida problems still unsettled, with every mail bringing more protests about impressment, and with British cargo seizures being confirmed in British prize courts, Jefferson's lot was not a happy one. In addition to all this burden, it appeared to Madison and Jefferson that their intentions were being misread in London and Paris. "The love of peace which we sincerely feel and profess, has begun to produce an opinion in Europe that our government is entirely in Quaker principles," Jefferson lamented.[14]

The year 1806 was hardly a time for the United States to seek the quiet refuge of a pacifist harbor. Nelson's victory at Trafalgar in October, 1805, left Napoleon landlocked and desperate for a means to counteract British sea power. His answer was the Berlin Decree (see Document 5-a), a blockade that tightened the vise on neutral shipping by forbidding neutrals to clear British ports. Meanwhile, an American negotiating team in London pressed for concessions from the British on impressment and trade, armed with a nonimportation act which, if permitted to go into effect, would strike at English commerce. When the negotiations appeared to promise a modicum of success, Jefferson postponed the effective date of the law aimed at British importations, but when the final treaty draft failed to promise an end to impressment but only offered "immediate and prompt redress" for the rights of American citizens, the document was doomed. Jefferson refused to send the treaty to the Senate, and when news of the Order in Council of January 1807 reached America the conferences between Madison and Jefferson were overcast with gloom.

## The Policy of Economic Retaliation: The Embargo Act

The humiliating *Chesapeake* affair in June, 1807, when the British man-of-war *Leopard* raked the American warship after a demand for British deserters had been refused, brought the nation's public men and media to a war chant. At that moment, if Jefferson had called Congress to hear a war message, "he would have had war at the drop of a hat; and it would have been a far more popular and successful war than the one finally declared in 1812."[15] Well might Woodrow Wilson have recalled this incident when he spoke of a nation being "too proud to fight," but at the moment even the Federalists in Boston were amazed at the audacity of the British navy. Still, Madison counseled forbearance and Jefferson practiced it, so that London received not an ultimatum but a demand for reparations and an end to impressment (*Alternative 4*: see Documents 4-a and 4-b). England answered Napoleon with a shocking "paper blockade" that ordered neutrals to steer clear of any European port under French control (see Document 5-b). Meanwhile, Jefferson's retaliation came in the Embargo Act of December 1807 (see Document 5-c), which along with the early nonimportation law placed a lock on the entrance to every American harbor. Henceforth, American ships were to stay out of foreign ports, all exports to foreign countries were prohibited, and a list of British goods was declared boycotted.

If the British and French were determined to destroy American commerce they would have to invade the United States to carry out their plans, for no ship flying the United States flag could be legally involved in international trade.

In this fashion Madison joined with Jefferson in believing that economic coercion would bring the two major powers to their senses. But at the heart of the problem was the Republican belief that unless the depredations on American commerce were halted, American nationality was gravely threatened. Whether Madison and Jefferson ever indulged in prayer or not is uncertain, but surely at this moment they must have either prayed or wished most powerfully that both France and England would feel such a squeeze from their merchants and hard-pressed citizens that the Orders in Council and Berlin Decree would be revoked (*Alternative 2:* see Documents 5-a and 5-b). They were not rescinded, however, and from the barrage of criticism unleashed towards the Republicans in New England it was clear that the Embargo Act was foredoomed. The result was a stagnation of commerce, rotting ships in harbors from Charleston to Nantucket, and a political division of the country that transcended any outcries since the days of the Alien and Sedition Acts.

Madison's difficulties were compounded by Jefferson's mental state during his last six months in office. Once it was determined that Madison would be his successor, Jefferson all but took his hand off the tiller and allowed the ship of state to drift during the rest of his term. Convinced that the embargo had failed because of New England duplicity (or worse, possibly treason in Jefferson's view), the president thought that the only alternative to continuation of the ban on maritime commerce was a shooting war. Neither Madison nor Jefferson wanted a war with either of the major European belligerents, but they were reluctant to admit that the embargo had been a gross failure (*Alternative 4:* see Documents 6-a and 6-b). It may be fair to say that at this stage in their long relationship, the two men were actually too close to each other to understand the kind of action needed to avert further damage to the nation. Madison, even if he knew what should have been done, was reluctant to push his old friend during the period of his "lame duck" administration. But Madison also was limited in his future course of action—he could not deviate radically from the Republican program he had helped design (see Document 6).[16]

In the circumstances, Albert Gallatin was more of a realist than Madison dared to be. He wrote a report which Representative G. W. Campbell of Tennessee carried to the House on November 22, 1808, that delineated the problems confronting the nation. The British Orders in Council and French decrees had amounted to "a maritime war waged by both nations against the United States. It cannot be denied that the ultimate and only effectual mode of resisting that warfare, if persisted in, is war."

This was saber-rattling, indeed, but none of the forthright proposals made by administration supporters made headway. Finally, a plan from Wilson Cary Nicholas of Virginia calling for repeal of the embargo and the use of force to meet force on the high seas—"the logical capstone to the structure that Gallatin and his friends desired"—foundered in Congress.[17] The loyal Republicans drew back, and Nicholas told Madison that the "only honorable course was from Embargo to war" (see Document 8-b) but the votes for even a tougher policy were lacking.

Although Madison had been a kind of godfather to the embargo, his own reputation was spared during the ensuing debacle through a variety of fortuitous circumstances.[18] The Federalists swept office after office in New England during the backlash of criticism, when by the most explicit statements Boston newspapers warned that Jefferson had made a covenant with Napoleon which included the embargo. But the Federalists could not unite on a candidate who had some Republican support, and finally nominated Charles Cotesworth Pinckney. Angry New York Republicans shoved George Clinton forward as an antiadministration nominee, while a faction of "pure Republicans" chose James Monroe. In the circumstances, Madison emerged from a congressional caucus as the regular Republican nominee and was elected as Jefferson's successor. The din of dissent was growing, however, and in the last days of Jefferson's second term the obnoxious embargo was officially declared a blunder when Congress passed its repeal only three days before Madison was inaugurated. The repeal was part of a Nonintercourse Act that narrowed trade prohibitions to the belligerents, closed American ports to their vessels, and left the door open for a renewal of trade with any power recognizing American maritime rights (*Alternative 2:* see Document 8-c).

## Notes

1. Irving Brant, *James Madison, Secretary of State, 1800-1809* (Indianapolis: Bobbs Merrill, 1953), p. 331.
2. Henry Adams, *History of the Administration of Jefferson and Madison,* 9 vols. (Boston, 1891-96), vol. 5. p. 39.
3. Ibid., p. 127.
4. Irving Brant, *James Madison, Nationalist, 1780-1787* (Indianapolis: Bobbs Merrill, 1948), p. 34.
5. Brant, Madison, *Secretary of State,* p. 527; Adams, *History,* vol. 5, p. 11.
6. Samuel Eliot Morison and Henry S. Commager, *The Growth of the American Republic,* 2 vols. (New York: Oxford University Press, 1956), vol. 1, p. 408.
7. Bradford Perkins, *Prologue to War, England and the United States* (Berkeley: University of California Press, 1968), p. 43.
8. Ralph Ketcham, *James Madison* (New York: Macmillan Co., 1971), p. 482.
9. John Quincy Adams, *The Lives of James Madison and James Monroe* (Buffalo, 1850), p. 173.
10. Ibid., p. 115.
11. Perkins, *Prologue to War,* p. 57.
12. Dumas Malone, *Jefferson the President, Second Term, 1805-1809* (Boston: Little, Brown & Co., 1974), p. 95.
13. Brant, Madison, *Secretary of State,* p. 303.
14. Perkins, *Prologue to War,* p. 121.
15. Morison and Commager, *The Growth of the American Republic,* vol. 1, p. 403.

16. Perkins, *Prologue to War*, p. 227, argues otherwise. He states that Madison as president-elect was free to "launch a new policy." The thinking of Jefferson and Madison was so much in the same channel that by this time Madison had not the independent judgment which would have led to innovative efforts for a new direction in United States foreign policy.

17. Ibid., p. 228.

18. Brant, *Madison, Secretary of State*, pp. 400-401.

# 3

# A Sincere Desire for Peace

By every external sign, except his height, Madison was the perfect embodiment of a president. None of his predecessors was as clear-thinking and able to grasp the central issue in a contentious situation, and in one sense Madison's experience and training since 1776 had prepared him for the honor bestowed on him on March 4, 1809. Nonetheless, during Madison's heavy involvement in national affairs over three decades he had accumulated enemies who were determined to exploit what was regarded as a certain character flaw in the new president. Madison, *un homme médiocre* to a French diplomat, was regarded as *un homme timide* by his adversaries. They intended to exploit what appeared to be Madison's chief weakness—his lack of courage.

One man's cowardice may be another man's prudence, so there is no need to apologize for Madison's political flaws. Indeed, he suffered excessively from a misdirected sense of loyalty, and he often suffered fools either gladly or indiscreetly (see Document 7). But few presidents in our history have demonstrated fitness for leadership while their relations with Congress were strained. The harmony needed at the two extremes of Pennsylvania Avenue for genuine effectiveness was notably absent in 1809, when Madison was reduced almost to a cipher by the machinations of men who were nominally Republicans and presumably loyal party men. Except for a few loyal and personal friends in Congress, Madison had left the inaugural ball as a president in search of a party, so that for a time it appeared that the country was adrift with only a caretaker in the White House.

The appointment of a cabinet illustrated Madison's dilemma. He wanted Gallatin as his chief aide, in the State Department, to serve as he had served Jefferson. But the president had two determined enemies in fellow Virginian William Branch Giles and another southern senator—Samuel Smith of Maryland. The main reason for their opposition to Gallatin as secretary of state may have been a deep-rooted sense of envy, for clearly the Swiss-born Pennsylvanian was superior to both in talent and energy. But their excuse for the rancor they showed at the mention of Gallatin's name was his foreign background, a xenophobic tendency often exhibited as the last refuge of scoundrels. At any rate, neither Giles nor Smith wished Madison or Gallatin well.

The delicacy of the situation bore upon Madison's later conduct of foreign affairs, for he needed all the help he could obtain from men of judgment and experience. On these counts Gallatin was the logical choice for the secretary of state, but the Giles-Smith faction broadcast its whispers shamelessly. "A party which had once trusted Burr and which still trusted Wilkinson, not to mention Giles, himself," Henry Adams observed, "had little right to discuss Gallatin's patriotism, or the honesty of foreign-born citizens."[1] Yet question Gallatin they did, and ultimately Madison set aside his trusted friend, Gallatin, in favor of a suspicious incompetent, Robert Smith (who happened to be Senator Smith's brother). Although Madison avoided a fight over his right as president to pick his cabinet, he compromised in the wrong direction. From the outset, he weighed his administration down with an inept political choice. As Madison later confessed, Smith was a deadweight in the State Department who could not be trusted either to write dispatches or even carry on a conversation in diplomatic circles, once the topic extended beyond the weather.

Perhaps Madison thought that the first days of his administration were not propitious for a battle over who really ran the country. Unfortunately, Gallatin remained a target for the dissidents after Madison made him secretary of the treasury, so that the conniving of ambitious or jealous men continued, while Gallatin made it clear that he could not be both a diplomat and a tax collector. He settled into the treasury building faster than Madison would have liked. Still, Madison observed the forms and tried to make it appear that Smith was an able public servant.[2] The appointment of Smith is only important here as an illustration of one of Madison's main problems—he was a chief of state with a household full of mediocre men and (owing to political pressures) unable to depend upon the most able member of his cabinet. There is no gainsaying the fact that if Gallatin had been Madison's secretary of state from March 5, 1809, onward, the foreign policy issues would have been better understood and more capably handled. This is not to say that Gallatin would have ultimately guided Madison away from a Napoleonic snare toward a peaceful solution, but at least Gallatin was a well-informed man of broad understanding with a judicious sense of what had to be done about America's humiliating international dilemma.

## Hopes and Pitfalls in Diplomatic Negotiations

Although the embargo had proved temporarily disastrous—with the price of cotton chopped almost in half and the Yankee seamen desperate for work—Madison could not have been unaware of the boost afforded to American manufacturers by the Republican policy of commercial retaliation. As Henry Adams pointed out, cotton prices recovered somewhat as New Englanders began to invest in spinning mills. Profits of one hundred and three hundred percent were recorded in the textile mills along the northern streams that provided the necessary water power. "All the Northern and Eastern States shared in the advantages of this production, for which Virginia with the Western and Southern States paid; but in the whole Union New England faired best," Adams observed.[3] Adams concluded that as the planters suffered, "while Virginia slowly sank into ruin," the northern mill owners recognized the profits which skyrocketed under the Republican programs of nonimportation and later of nonintercourse.

Nonetheless, the New England press pounded Madison mercilessly over the Nonintercourse Act, (see Document 8-c) and smuggling was openly countenanced on the Canadian border. Still Madison believed in the righteousness of the various courses pursued since 1803, and in April, 1809, after being in office a scant six weeks, Madison wrote a letter addressed to David Erskine, British envoy in Washington, which accepted the British offer of reparations for the *Chesapeake* affair. Written by Madison, but signed by Smith, the letter was somewhat ambiguous in sidestepping a protest of the Nonintercourse Act but explicit in its chagrin that the British officer commanding the *Leopard* had not been punished. As Henry Adams noted, the final sentence which Madison added was only a means of twisting the lion's tail, which is exactly what happened (see Document 9). "But I have it in express charge from the President to state that while he forbears to insist on the further punishment of the offending officer, he is not the less sensible of the justice and utility of such an example, nor the less persuaded that it would best comport with what is due from his Britannic Majesty to his own honor," the offending sentence read. Erskine, the British minister who accepted the note and thus ran the risk of royal ire, was a friendly diplomat who had come to America full of goodwill and a desire to heal all the wounds. The British foreign secretary read the sentence in a rage, while George III is said to have turned red over the passage—how impudent of an American president to lecture the king on what the honor of England demanded! Thus Madison had indiscreetly thrown up a roadblock on the path to an Anglo-American détente, and the unfortunate Erskine paid for the president's patronizing tone. As for Madison himself, Henry Adams insisted that the president "never understood that he had given cause of offence."[4]

At the time, however, Erskine was so anxious to keep peace hopes alive that he willingly overlooked Madison's little lecture and pushed for a more fundamental understanding. With the *Chesapeake* business thought to be out of the way, the great remaining obstacle was not impressment—though that was provocation enough to some westerners in the corridors of Congress—but rather the Orders in Council. What followed was a diplomatic mixup that proved embarrassing to all parties and ultimately left Madison with but two alternatives—acceptance of what almost amounted to a British protectorate, (*Alternative 3m*,: see Document 9) or a declaration of war (*Alternative 4*: see Document 15).

Modern writers have not agreed on how sincere Madison was as he entered into the negotiations with Erskine. A.L. Burt infers that Madison had misled Erskine once before by assuring the British minister that the Embargo Act "was not to be regarded as in any way tinged with hostility," and thus some fifteen months earlier Madison had made "professions of innocence . . . but they rang hollow."[5] Had Madison practiced duplicity on Erskine late in 1807, and was he preparing to practice it again? Without saying so, Brant intimates that Madison was following this intention by secretly committing the country to a war on a quid pro quo basis with either France or England while holding a series of talks with Erskine. For, acting upon the president's orders, Secretary Smith had sent dispatches to the American envoys in Paris and London authorizing them to offer secretly a pledge of a declarat'on of war against their enemy if either power would lift its decrees unconditionally. "Thus before Madison had been two weeks in office he had put the full weight of the Presidency behind a secret understanding with either England or France, involving a call for war against the other unless it too stopped molesting American commerce," Brant noted. "Secrecy was imperative at the time, but its end result was to help build a totally erroneous conception of Madison as President."[6] Bradford Perkins tended to view the whole business with contempt. "Neither Britain nor France, nor the American government itself, can have taken this very seriously," Perkins decided. "For the Americans, the conversations with ... Erskine ... offered far more promise."[7]

Madison had every reason to embrace the friendly overtures from Erskine. He had entered office faced with the embarrassment of an exposé in the Boston *Columbian Centinel* of secret letters between Madison (as secretary of state) and the American minister in France, John Armstrong. Shortly before Madison's inauguration, the arch-Federalist *Centinel* printed these letters serially to portray the French in a most damaging light, and then for extra measure published two Madison-William Pinkney letters which indicated England was becoming more tractable. Taken together, the letters produced the distinct impression that British gestures of friendship and French indignities had been suppressed by Madison while he was at the State Department helm (see Document 7).[8]

Thus Madison had every reason to hope that the negotiations with Erskine would prove fruitful, and the damage done by his April 17 letter was some months in the future. Oblivious of the way British cabinet officers would react to that unfortunate document, Madison took Erskine at face value and was in turn deceived by the Englishman's well-intentioned but totally misleading handling of their discussions. The chief difficulty stemmed from Erskine's reluctance to lay before Madison all his instructions from England's foreign minister, Canning. Erskine had known Madison slightly as secretary of state, and had good reason to believe that Madison was tiring of the long process of negotiation. Madison had suggested to Erskine that the alternatives open to America were either a war with England (*Alternative 5*) or—should France remain adamant about the Continental System—an Anglo-American alliance aimed at France (*Alternative 3*). For his part, Erskine hinted that a change in British policy was likely, so that the detested Orders in Council would be revised in such a way as to benefit American commerce.[9] Once Madison was in the White House, saddled with a new Nonimportation Act, Erskine had to report that the extensive revisions of the Orders were in fact only token gestures. The Orders still maintained that American ships headed for Europe must first pass through English ports or suffer condemnation. Since Napoleon's Milan Decree of 1807 held that American ships which had touched English ports en route to the Continent were subject to seizure, the American ship captain was still at the mercy of men-of-war flying either the tri-color or the Union Jack, while ships under the stars-and-stripes were hapless victims. In such a squeeze play, America was treated as something less than a sovereign power. Was she a second-class power? Third class?

Perhaps with misgivings, Madison looked back on the *Chesapeake* incident as a lost opportunity, for while his wife was still arranging the furniture in the presidential mansion, Madison began to perceive that a dangerous split was damaging the country internally. The New England Federalists were firing oral salvos on the new president, and though not quite as vituperative as those missiles reserved for Jefferson, there was too much malice in their criticism to leave Madison unmoved. Petitions from New England towns poured into Washington, begging for relief from the restrictive legislation that kept ships in port while goods lay piled on wharves. The leading Federalists were asking each other "whether the states to the east of the Delaware might not combine for the purpose of preventing a war against Great Britain," and the Force Act early in 1809 had caused four thousand angry citizens to converge on Faneuil Hall as ships in the Boston harbor hoisted black flags at half-mast.[10] To cap it all, the stronghold of the Republicans above the Potomac was slipping, a fact confirmed by the election of a high priest of the Federalists, Christopher Gore, as governor of Massachusetts early in April.

## Attempt at Détente: The Erskine Incident

Madison's luck was still holding, however, for the bad news from Boston had barely reached his ears when Erskine reported that a new set of instructions had arrived from London which authorized a final settlement of all Anglo-American differences. The *Chesapeake* affair was settled but, as noted earlier, Madison overplayed the last scene and in fact helped bring the curtain down with a crash. At the moment, however, Madison failed to resist the temptation to expose the British as opportunists with no real regard for international law unless it fitted their purposes. And Erskine, all too eager to report a diplomatic triumph to his home office, passed over the *Chesapeake* note as a nightmare. What Erskine's zeal also led him to do was far more distressing to Canning, who had admonished his representative in America that the Orders in Council would be revoked provided three conditions were met: (1) all American prohibitions on commerce affecting England should be dropped but kept in force against France; (2) the Rule of 1756 prohibiting colonial trade in enemy ports during hostilities should be recognized as valid by the Americans; and (3) the Americans should concede to England the right to seize any American ships complying with the Continental System under Napoleon's decrees. Most damaging of all, however, was the wrap kept over Canning's prefactory note which explained that these conditions *had to be met prior to a revocation of the Orders in Council*. Erskine's secret proviso was meant to be exhibited, but was not shown to either Madison or Secretary of State Smith. Hurriedly, Smith and Madison perused Erskine's letter, conceded his first point, quibbled about the second, and rejected the third.

Gallatin was suspicious and Smith was confused by the sudden reversal of British truculence. Only two days after the sharp letter on the *Chesapeake* affair had been sealed, Smith hurried off to tell Erskine that the president was willing to exercise his authority and declare the Nonintercourse Act repealed insofar as England was concerned "on the 10th of June next" (see Documents 9-a and 9-b). That was enough for Erskine, who brushed the second and third conditions aside with a promise that England would drop the Orders as soon as the news reached Whitehall. The next move was an official proclamation, which Madison gave to his friend Samuel Harrison Smith for publication in the proadministration newspaper, the *National Intelligencer*.[11] Smith printed the official revocation, along with all the Erskine-Smith correspondence. The total effect of this news was electrifying. Federalists were dumbfounded and then delirious, while ardent Republicans believed that the forbearing policies of Jefferson and Madison had been vindicated.

In retrospect, Madison regretted his precipitous rush to reopen the trade with England. Although he had not seen Erskine's official instructions, he assumed that Erskine was competent to make promises which carried the heaviest implications, for if the détente went into effect a war with France would most likely result (*Alternative 3*: see Documents 9-b and 9-d). "For the moment Madison was the most popular President that ever had met Congress. At no session since 1789 had such harmony prevailed as during the five weeks of this political paradise," Adams observed.[12] The outcry over impressments was muted in the special session as bills went through Congress implementing Madison's proclamation. All that was needed was a confirmation from London of the arrangement.

Those whose memory goes back to the frustrating negotiations between the Vietnamese belligerents over the shape of tables at a diplomatic conference, an argument that consumed precious days while blood was being spilled, must know that the maze of diplomacy has always been a slow, tortuous pathway. In 1809 Madison himself tended to forget this, and he was culpable for this error, since he had so recently served as secretary of state, when he precipitated a crisis by naively taking Erskine's assurances at face value. With some justice Henry Adams chastised Madison for proceeding to issue a far-reaching proclamation suspending the Nonintercourse Act on the assumption that the ministry in London would support Erskine, "and without even asking to see the British negotiator's special powers or instruction."[13] This was alacrity, indeed, and Madison exposed his flank to both Francophiles and his own party's chief critics (see Document 9-c) by pretending that the British had been outmaneuvered—that in fact the embargo had forced England into the very position the two Republican presidents insisted she would eventually accept.

What made the Erskine incident all the more embarrassing was the effort Republican newspapers made to exploit the apparent triumph. While canny old John Tyler (Madison's long-time acquaintance, now the Virginia governor) reacted with the rest of the nation in measured glee, Tyler cautioned that "this mighty Victory [was] obtain'd by foreign events more than our Country's firmness or British morality" (Tyler to Madison, April 24, 1809). This backhanded praise was hardly the kind of message Madison longed to receive, for his policy was built on the belief that the chief cause of British flexibility was American firmness—that is, the embargo.

Then a succession of bombshells fell into Madison's lap. It could be argued with great plausibility that upon receipt of two unexpectedly harsh news dispatches from London the only preventative for an Anglo-American war would have been the collapse of Napoleon. First, a new British Order in Council dated April 26, 1809, arrived in Washington in midsummer (see Document 9-d). It rescinded the old Order demanding that American ships carrying enemy goods first clear British ports, but at the same time decreed that all continental ports, from Holland to Italy, were under an official blockade. Thus, any American vessels bound to or from that area were subject to seizure by the British navy. All trade with French or Dutch colonies was prohibited under the Rule of 1756.

How could Erskine's authority have been so broad, if the British were still in such a bellicose mood? Perhaps Erskine had been less than candid. "The puzzle created by the Order of April [26] struck every one," Madison wrote Jefferson, hoping against hope that Erskine's promises would prove valid (Madison to Jefferson, June 20, 1809). Perhaps in half-dread that the worst news was still in store, the Madisons packed up and left for their summer vacation at Montpelier, but two weeks later the president was forced to leave Virginia and return to Washington (see Document 9-e). By a "mortifying" mixture of British "fraud and folly," Erskine's agreement had been repudiated. The stride toward a détente had reached Canning on May 22, and three days later London newspapers trumpeted: Erskine's olive branch had been rejected by the foreign minister (Document 9-f).

Madison hardly concealed his disappointment as he ordered the Nonintercourse Act redirected against England in August, 1809. Erskine packed his bags to return home in official disgrace, reprimanded for having exceeded his authority. At the same time, the British tried to make it appear that Madison knew of the restrictions on Erskine's power to negotiate and had pulled off a coup simply to exasperate the British.[14] All the evidence points the other way, however (see Document 9-g). Madison was not told the whole story by Erskine, whose chief offense was his anxiety to make headway toward a peaceful settlement of the outstanding differences. Madison had acted in good faith, but the British took the opposite to be true by hinting at a certain duplicity on the part of his administration.

## A Diplomacy of Bad Faith

On top of this insulting attitude, Canning had heaped another blunder by choosing Francis James Jackson as Erskine's successor. Jackson's name is almost lost now in the dustbin of obscurity, but when his selection as the

American minister was revealed, Jackson's reputation as a diplomatic "hit man" was widespread. Jackson had been sent to Denmark in 1807 as an envoy carrying a direct threat to the Danish people, and after his humiliating ultimatum was delivered the British navy had pounded Copenhagen until the Danes sued for peace. Thereafter, the name of "Copenhagen" Jackson was associated with the crudest sort of diplomacy. Now he was bound for America on the heels of Erskine's disgrace. A poorer choice could hardly have been made by Canning, unless he wished to use Jackson in a war of nerves in preference to one of weapons (see Document 10). Jackson's instructions were a study in nineteenth-century diplomatic syntax—he was to do nothing but do it with finesse—and the minister's impression could only have been that he was sent to America not to initiate serious talks, but rather to allow matters to simmer for a while.

The selection of Jackson was abrasive enough, but public disclosure of Erskine's full instructions by Canning made the whole diplomatic maze more enigmatic. Madison had nourished the belief that somehow the latest Orders in Council were not as insulting as they appeared—that some new step was about to be taken in London which would explain how Erskine could have been so misleading. With the latest revelations, however, "Canning's course on one side [of] the Atlantic seemed so little to accord with his tactics on the other, that neither party could longer believe in the other's good faith," Henry Adams concluded. "For the first time in this contest, Englishmen and Americans could no longer understand each other's meaning."[15] A dangerous stage in the negotiations had now been reached, for leaders in both nations seemed convinced of the other's bad faith. Since an exchange of notes between London and Washington took at least four weeks, given fair wind and good weather, it must have occurred to Madison and to the British (who were having cabinet difficulties that led, among other problems, to a duel between the former secretaries of foreign affairs and war) that war might come momentarily through some unforeseen incident.

From this time onward, Madison took few pains to conceal his chagrin with the British. Jackson was forced to await the president's pleasure before an official reception could take place. He spent some of this time reviewing all the correspondence between his predecessor and the Americans. Jackson was amazed, complained at being forced "to wade through such a mass of folly and stupidity," and concluded that Madison and his cabinet had made a fool of Erskine with their repeated saber-rattlings. "Every third word was a declaration of war," Jackson sighed.[16]

Canning left office during the fall of 1809 amidst the general disarray around Whitehall, but Madison expected no improvement. "The change in the Ministry seems likely to make bad worse," Madison wrote Jefferson, while Jackson had proved himself "a worthy instrument of his patron, Canning" (Madison to Jefferson, Nov. 6, 1809). By November 8, further talks with Jackson seemed pointless, and he was told curtly and officially to go home (see Document 10-b). Jackson was shaken, but remained arrogantly confident that all the blame for his failure fell upon Madison.

In a time when the president's annual message to Congress was one of the most important stories to come from Washington, usually reprinted in full in nearly every newspaper from Wall Street to the end of the Natchez Trail, Madison's first "State of the Union" report was eagerly awaited. Somber in tone, the message recounted the failure of Erskine's mission, the reimposition of the Nonintercourse Act, and intimated that better times in Anglo-American relations were as distant as ever. Madison scarcely mentioned France, except to infer that the situation in Paris was almost as bleak as in London. His Republican conscience twinged by the falling customs receipts (this main source of government revenue was bound to plunge as international commerce abated), Madison hinted at a deficit in the next budget, yet hoped for some military expenditures that would reinforce the sternness of American diplomacy. The paradox of a Republican president appealing for financial sustenance for a war machine was scarcely missed by Madison's opponents in Congress, such as John Randolph, who were determined to block any large outlays to public money for either more ships or an increased army.[17]

## Abandoning the Policy of Economic Retaliation: Steps Toward War

There is reason to believe that Madison was on a course toward war after the fall of 1809, for he was convinced of the bad faith of the British and had no expectation that Napoleon could relax his predatory policies. In the full flush of the Erskine agreement it seemed that the policy of economic retaliation had been vindicated, but after that euphoric moment dissolved in the realities of Canning's rancor, surely Madison realized that—barring a sudden peace in Europe, which nobody foresaw—the United States would have to surrender all her claims to national sovereignty, leave her citizens and her ships to the mercy of the major powers, and walk humbly among the mighty.

At the moment, there was no other choice left for Madison. The army was in a chaotic state, a much-touted gunboat experiment had ended in a failure, and the purse strings held by squabbling congressmen were hardly to be loosened for armaments. There seems to have been no clear understanding either on Capitol Hill or in the White House that in Europe the only factor that counted in diplomacy was the number of ships of the line, the size of an army, and the firepower of its weapons. Might indeed made all things right by the Napoleonic dictum, and thus America was almost impotent at the conference table in such circumstances.

To make matters worse, Madison had only Gallatin left as a dependable ally. Determined to push Americans to a course of action, the astute secretary of the treasury drafted a bill which would at least allow American merchantmen to go out in search of cargoes while closing home ports to belligerent men-of-war. Known as Macon's Bill No. 1, the measure became enshrouded in partisan politics, as some Federalists feared the result would be a war with England, while others believed it would reopen trade routes with Great Britain. Finally, the bill was pigeonholed by a hopeless deadlock between the House and the Senate. A second measure, also bearing Macon's name, limped through Congress to passage as admittedly the best of a series of bad bargains. "The Senate and House of Representatives act in such entire harmony that when the one says I will the other says I wont," a partisan observer reported.[18] The upshot was that all parties tended to place their own interpretation on Macon's Bill No. 2 (see Document 10-f). Critics thought it placed national honor on the auction block, while its friends thought its removal of all restrictions on American commerce served notice that the flag would fly wherever daring men could take it. Madison regarded the bill with less than enthusiasm, although it empowered the president to impose trade restrictions (a nonintercourse law) against one belligerent if the other revoked all its punitive decrees.

What disturbed Madison most about Macon's Bill No. 2 was its clear abandonment of his and Jefferson's policy of economic retaliation (*Alternative 4*: see Document 10-c).[19] By throwing all American ports open the bill would ensure the British monopoly of shipping and commerce in major United States ports. Predictably, when this happened those British manufacturers who had protested the Orders in Council changed their tactics and "the clamor . . . subsided to a whisper."[20] American commodities were soon stacked high on English wharves as the prices paid for staples from the southern states plummeted. The monopoly thus granted to the British shippers and merchants hit American pocketbooks directly. "Cotton I perceive is down at 10 or 11 cents in Georgia. The great mass of Tobacco is in a similiar situation. And the effect must soon be general, with the exception of a few articles which do not at present, glut the British demand," the president wrote bitterly (see Document 10-d). Meanwhile, the American minister in France sent home word that the French were recklessly confiscating American goods and ships. "This scene on the continent, and the effect of English monopoly on the value of our produce," Madison surmised, proved the inefficacy of Macon's Bill No. 2. However, in Madison's mind there was no doubt as to the chief offender. Between British selfishness and French rapacity, "public attention is beginning to fix itself on the proof it affords that the original sin agst. Neutrals lies with G. B. & that whilst she acknowledges it, she persists in it" (see Document 10-f).

Madison knew that France was also trampling on American rights, but between the two major powers he had no doubts about the one most interested in throttling American expansion. Moreover, in the way the Congress had left matters, there was a way left for Napoleon to take advantage of any tendency to favor the French. Since the law allowed the president to lift all restrictions on whichever belligerent withdrew its edicts against neutral commerce, Napoleon contrived to produce the needed documents without bothering to implement them. In other words, he would force Madison to suspend all commercial laws directed against France merely by announcing "that the decrees of Berlin and Milan are revoked, and that after November 1 they will cease to have effect . . .,"(see Documents 11 and 11-a). Napoleon had by a stroke of his pen set a snare which Madison could only avoid by calling Napoleon a liar, unless the British bailed him out of trouble by announcing that the Orders in Council would also be revoked on November 1. But Napoleon calculated that the British would not alter their course, and his own plan was to instruct the Duke of Cadore to hand the American minister a note and await the American reaction.

Madison's next moves have been condemned by several historians as flagrant abuses of presidential power, and defended by his biographers as justifiable exercises of executive authority. Burt indicated that Madison either fell into a trap or leaped into it, while Perkins calculated that the president wanted to keep Napoleon involved in a fishing expedition "without swallowing the visible hook."[21] Brant skirted all charges of ineptness or deceit and treated the president's reaction straightforwardly; Madison proceeded in the belief that Napoleon meant what he said, and the cynical if not deceitful acts of the French emperor were not then apparent (see Document 11-b). Perkins tempered his criticism by saying that the president acted hastily— informing England that the decrees had been revoked and that the intercourse acts would be reemployed against the British without waiting for confirmation that Napoleon was keeping his word. When the American minister in France offered no evidence that Napoleon was indeed relenting (see Document 11-c), Madison still pushed ahead and on November 2, announced that the French would now be exempted from commercial restrictions on American commerce (see Document 11-d). Possibly the British thought the president could not be so naive as to accept Napoleon's assurances without looking into the actual situation, although their official reaction was that when proof of a French revocation came to hand they would revoke the Orders in Council. This reply from Lord Wellesley was viewed by Madison with suspicions he had not shown toward French pronouncements, a course of conduct which Perkins thought might be explained by the president's personality. "Perhaps in part because he had suffered such deep humiliation through the Erskine agreement, James Madison refused to admit that he had erred.'[22]

Indeed, there is also evidence to suggest that Madison decided to take Napoleon at his word because the American minister in France did nothing to contradict the French claims. Madison impatiently awaited news from Armstrong that would have played a significant role in his assessment of Napoleon's sincerity. Armstrong, however, "lent himself readily to the silence that was needed." Somehow he must have known that while Napoleon was holding the Cadore letter in one hand he was aware that about fifty American cargoes in Dutch, Spanish, and other French-occupied ports were then in the process of being sold for the benefit of the French treasury. Yet Armstrong may have wanted to close his diplomatic career in triumph, as Adams believed, so he avoided any confrontation with Cadore and let Madison assume that all was proceeding well in the French capital.[23]

## Juggling France and England

No doubt the late summer and autumn were a vexing time for Madison, for he longed for good news from Armstrong, and although none came, he had already committed the nation to a course of action. Still there is something to be said for Madison's dilemma. The Cadore letter was so skillfully composed that had Madison rejected it outright American vessels would have been caught in another embargo—for Madison still thought a patient republic could outlast the outrages of the two great powers. And although Napoleon privately dismissed the note as a meaningless commitment, the honor of the French nation stood behind it in the court of world opinion; indeed, not until secret information came to light some years later was his complete Machiavellianism manifested. Moreover, every American president is answerable for his errors at the polling place, so Madison knew that if he was walking into a French ambush he would have to justify his conduct at the next election. Thus if Madison deserved Adams's harsh hindsight judgment—that by issuing a proclamation the president thereby "made himself a party to Napoleon's fraud"—the voters in 1812 would have the final judgment.

In one sense, Madison was serving notice on England that the United States had decided that between the two belligerents, the French were the least damaging to American commerce (see Documents 11-c and 11-d). This was no high compliment, but neither was it a proclamation tantamount to war; and except for the Federalist chieftans and their newspaper allies, the presidential proclamation was received by Americans with some sense of relief. The flip-flop tactics of the Federalists had cost them a number of seats in the congressional elections during the summer and fall of 1810, and an assertive band of younger men strode into the halls of Congress early in December, with Henry Clay, John C. Calhoun, Felix Grundy, and William Lowndes in the forefront. If Madison's old adversaries in Congress had been too provincial to be ambitious nationally, the newer men were too ambitious to have local views. The congressmen heard in the president's second annual message (see Document 11-h) that the revocation of the Milan and Berlin decrees was an indisputable fact, but Madison admitted that the sequestered property of Americans known to be in French hands had not been restored. The occupation of West Florida, carried on by Americans and recognized by the president, was duly noted as a legitimate exercise of American power. Some trouble with Denmark's "licentious cruisers" was reported (see Document 10-a), and the amicable settlement with the Barbary states was worth a sentence. Otherwise, the thrust of the president's speech was pointed more to domestic accomplishments and internal affairs. Nothing in this speech indicated that a warlike spirit pervaded the administration, and the last thing Madison was prepared to do was admit that he had acted hastily in accepting Napoleon's assurances that the edicts supporting the Continental System no longer applied to the United States. Most presidents have loathed admitting their mistakes, and Madison was too much a politician and far too conscious of the presidential burden to have been an exception.

Armstrong's replacement in France, Jonathan Russell, soon began sending home dispatches that bore out all the contentions of the president's critics that France was still seizing American ships and confiscating cargoes. Napoleon's rule was that once an American ship had touched an English port she became fair game for the French, and thus an important segment of American commerce was continuously jeopardized while on the high seas. The British demanded proof that the ship was making an uninterrupted voyage to an English harbor or it was liable for seizure, while the French insisted that a British endorsement on the landing papers made the cargo subject to French reprisals. It is something of a tribute to the audacity of American shipmasters and seamen that hundreds of vessels cleared their home ports and ran innumerable risks in search of profits for Yankee merchant princes. Still, the fact remained that American ships, captured by the French on the pretext of trade with Napoleon's enemy, were rotting in their European berths (see Document 11-f).

Madison apparently had no faith in the efficacy of prayer, yet he must have wished mightily for some indication that Napoleon's word was not worthless. Saddled with the inept Robert Smith in the State Department, Madison well knew how that office was conducted and doubtless spent many hours scanning reports from Europe in search of encouraging news. There was nothing, however, but disappointment coming in every dispatch case (see Document 11-a). Russell became disillusioned and lost all his fervor for the French cause, while consuls and charges in various ports repeated the sad story of jailed seamen, appeals from creditors, and sales of cargoes worth many thousands of dollars upon condemnation by British or French admiralty courts (see Document 11-c). A section in Macon's Bill No. 2 had a ninety-day cutoff provision on the trade restrictions directed against England, and thus legislation was required to renew the ban. A new nonintercourse bill came to the House with administration support and was promptly assailed by Federalists. Representative William Milnor tried to bell the cat with an exposé of Madison's position by reading Russell's letter to Cadore of December 10, 1810, remonstrating against the seizure of the American brig *New Orleans Packet* (see Document 11-f). "It is now evident that the President was duped by the French Emperor, and led to issue a proclamation on the faith of his promise, declaring a fact which did not exist."[24] By now this chant had become an old story, and most of the House was not listening. With cold logic, John Randolph had already demonstrated that Madison was in an untenable position, and suggested that if England had sequestered and sold cargoes and then justified the actions as a "retaliatory measure" after declaring its edicts revoked (as had the French), how would Congress react? "I ask whether we should not have war against that country in four and twenty hours?" Randolph answered his own query. "Unquestionably we would."[25]

## Notes

1. Henry Adams, *History of the Administration of Jefferson and Madison*, 9 vols. (Boston, 1891-96), vol. 5, p. 6.

2.  Bradford Perkins, *Prologue to War, England and the United States* (Berkeley: University of California Press, 1968), p. 269. Madison tried to live with Smith, only to find that Smith was both incompetent and treacherous. Even when it was clear that Smith had to be either fired or kicked into a diplomatic corner somewhere, Madison avoided an open rupture. For all his pains, Smith came back with a bitterness that soon spilled over in his *Address to the People* of the United States, a distorted account of Madison's years in public life. Smith's mendacity was so patent that the pamphlet harmed him far more than it damaged the president, although those who gleefully called Madison a Francophile cited Smith's screed as proof. But Smith's rancor boomeranged, as Perkins notes, in "one of the rare instances of a man's giving the finishing stroke to his character, in his eagerness to ruin the enemy."

3.  Adams, *History*, vol. 5, p. 17.

4.  Ibid., p. 70.

5.  A.L. Burt, *The United States, Great Britain and British North America from the Revolution to the Establishment of Peace after the War of 1812* (New York: 1961), p. 257.

6.  Irving Brant, *James Madison, the President, 1809-1812* (Indianapolis: Bobbs Merrill, 1957), p. 42.

7.  Perkins, *Prologue to War*, pp. 233-34.

8.  Brant, *Madison the President*, p. 38.

9.  Ibid., p. 35.

10. Helen R. Pinkney,   *Christopher Gore, Federalist of Massachusetts, 1758-1827* (Waltham, Mass.: Barre, 1969), pp. 111-12.

11. Adams, *History*, vol. 5, p. 73.

12. Ibid., p. 80.

13. Ibid., p. 74.

14. Burt, *The United States, Great Britain and British North America*, p. 276.

15. Adams, *History*, vol. 5, p. 113.

16. Ibid., p. 120.

17. Brant, *Madison, the President*, pp. 131-35.

18. Perkins, *Prologue to War*, p. 242.

19. Brant, *Madison, the President*, p. 138.

20. Perkins, *Prologue to War*, p. 244.

21. Burt, *The United States, Great Britain and British North America*, pp. 283-84; Perkins, *Prologue to War*, pp. 248-51.

22. Perkins, *Prologue to War*, p. 252.

23. Adams, *History*, vol. 5, pp. 259-60.

24. U.S., Congress, *Annals of Congress*, 11th Cong., 3d sess., 1810, pp. 999-1001.

25. Ibid., pp. 864-65.

# 4

# Willingness for War

Madison's embarrassment in the last days of 1810 and the beginning of 1811 must have been extreme, for he had worked his administration into a tight corner (see Document 11-h). "Only an uncharacteristic act of Napoleonic charity or abject British capitulation could provide a peaceful exit," Perkins surmised. "The ultimate alternative was war."[1] Yet the administration did not push for anything beyond renewal of the Nonintercourse Act with England, and won that handily in spite of the opposition's logical triumph—sixty-four to twelve in the House, and twenty to seven in the Senate (see Documents 12, 12-a, and 12-b).

## Watching and Waiting

The overwhelming majority for the administration bill, which legalized whatever fiction there was in the presidential proclamation, carried certain implications. Congress was prepared to accept Madison's version of the French revocations and paid little attention to any evidence to the contrary, not because there was a belief in Napoleon's integrity but because *a choice had already been made*. That decision was that England should have plenty of time to decide on canceling the Orders in Council, but if the war continued the alternative to revoking the Orders was war (*Alternative 5*: see Document 12-c) Surely this must have been in Madison's mind as he pressed for a clear-cut decision by the British cabinet on the issue. Since the new Nonintercourse Act had to be retroactive to February 2, 1811, some leniency was permitted to ship captains in reimposing the ban on British commerce. This was hardly the posture of a nation bent on war. As for a real turnabout in British thinking, however, Madison assumed the worst. "It would seem that G. B. is determined agst. repealing her orders, and that Bonaparte is equally so on the destruction on her commerce, to which he readily sacrifices his own commerce with the U. S.," he wrote Jefferson. He still harbored only the dimmest hope. "After all, we must remain somewhat in the dark till we hear more on the subject," he counseled (Madison to Jefferson, June 7, 1811).

This watchful waiting on Madison's part led his opponents to believe Madison was gripped with a severe case of doubt, as indeed he was, for it was in the president's nature to delay a painful decision as long as possible. More perhaps than any man in Washington, Madison knew that the cabinet was not fit for conducting a war, that the nation was not passionately demanding a fight, and the nation's state of preparedness was little short of shocking. Perhaps Madison's greatest flaw of character was his vacillation, but he was not vacillating out of timidity. If he appeared to waver, it was because there was little else he could do but follow an excruciating labyrinth. For in his own mind, Madison was still convinced that economic coercion ought to be given every test before it was abandoned for the only other alternative—war.

At this point we need to remind ourselves that all of the debate over foreign policy taking place in the United States was a unique situation in world experience. Nowhere but in the United States was the possibility of war so openly discussed, so many alternatives proposed, and administrative actions so widely criticized as in Congress, at dinner tables, and in newspaper columns. The very thing which Jefferson and Madison wanted—a full discussion of public policies so that the genius of the *vox populi* could come forth—all this was vexing Madison as it had his three predecessors. The thought that Napoleon would have countenanced such criticism brings a smile, and although the press in England was critical, in no other nation were the actions of the head of state subject to such public scrutiny. One effect of this republican approach to foreign affairs was to limit the courses of action open to the president. He had to pursue a program that would be popular while still doing what his judgment told him would serve the country best.

As a southerner facing a hostile New England electorate, Madison deserves deserves credit in that he never weighed an issue in terms of what effect it would have on one section of the country. Henry Adams's remark that the policies of Jefferson and Madison enriched the manufacturing states and ruined the staple-producing states was not meant to laud their patriotism, but no better proof can be found of their disinterestedness than this solemn Yankee historian's interpretation:

> The Federalist leaders and newspapers grumbled without intermission that their life-blood was drained to support a negro-slave aristocracy, "baser than its own slaves," as their phrase went; and what they could not clutch was taken by New York and Pennsylvania, while Virginia slowly sank into ruin. Virginia paid the price to gratify her passion for political power; and at the time she paid it knowingly and willingly.... American manufacturers owed more to Jefferson and Virginia, who disliked them, than to Northern statesmen, who merely encouraged them after they were established.[2]

What Adams was saying, in effect, was that the two Republican presidents pursued their policies disinterestedly, to the detriment of their own section, because their paramount concern was the maintenance of the Union. At the nub of every doubt in Madison's mind there was always the agonizing question: "Will this act strengthen or damage the Union?" (see Document 12-c).

Unfortunately, Madison gave the outward appearance of lacking resolution, since he was not a fighting president who was willing to use the newspapers and pamphlets to counteract the Federalists' onslaught. If one had read the Federalist newspapers in any major city, with Benjamin Russell playing the chief role as a president-baiter, the impression left was that Madison was the cat's-paw of a Francophile faction that was wantonly reeling toward a war against England. When Russell tired of denouncing the alleged follies of the administration, the Baltimore *Federal Republican* or the New York *Evening Post* picked up the president's scent and frequently borrowed the Bostonian's favorite smear word for the Madison administration—"Jacobinism."

Meanwhile, New England towns peppered the White House with petitions against reimposition of restrictions on British trade, and the suffering citizens of New Haven made an appeal that touched Madison's senitive nerve when they demanded a special session of Congress to repeal all commercial reprisals. Without alluding to the damaging effects of nonintercourse on his own state, Madison pointed out the effort made to force a revocation of depredations on neutral commerce. "If sacrifices made for the sake of the whole, result more to some than to other districts or descriptions of Citizens, this . . . is an effect which tho' always to be regreted, can never be entirely avoided. Whether the appeal be to the sword, or to interruptions or Modifications of customary intercourse, an equal operation on every part of the Community can never happen" (see Document 13-b).

Patience—restraint—forbearance—Madison's light touch made the opposition believe that the president was totally lacking in qualities of leadership, a judgment shared by not a few modern historians. "The appearance of weakness [in Madison] was as fatal to an effective exercise of presidential leadership as weakness itself," Perkins ventured.[3] Actually, Madison's enemies persistently underrated his abilities and historians have inclined to echo that judgment, but he was preparing a cabinet revolution after Congress adjourned in the spring of 1811 that at least would place the executive branch in readiness for the approaching war (see Document 13).

## Strengthening the Administration

Madison perceived the trend of public opinion in the way that his dear friend Jefferson could not (see Documents 12-c and 13-a). The sage of Monticello, sorting his seeds and recording the progress of his strawberry plants, was unaware of the concerns of the nation. Still convinced that he had been right all along with the embargo policy, and that Madison would carry the same plan forward insofar as he could, Jefferson told friends the people were ignoring the fiery editors and placing their reliance in the deliberate policies of the administration. The last two Congresses had provided plenty of bellicose statements "for printers thirsting after war, some against France and some against England. But the people wish for peace with both" (Jefferson to Monroe, May 5, 1811).[4]

Madison's own reading of the public pulse was different. He assumed that the people shared his own sense of disillusionment, and therefore Madison worked quietly and persistently toward the reconstruction of an administration which he undoubtedly realized had a narrow base. It was time for Madison to have more than Gallatin to rely upon. In the early spring, overtures were made to seek out better men, for it was obvious that rough seas were ahead and, with the likes of Robert Smith and Caesar Rodney on board, there was little intellectual ballast of the kind Madison needed.

In the circumstances, Madison had decided to fall back on an old friend and a fellow Virginian as the mainspring of the revitalized cabinet. Through a series of friendly overtures, Madison drew James Monroe forward with an expression that bygones were bygones (Monroe had been terribly interested in running for the presidency in 1808), and there had been too many rumors in the press to ignore the possibility of a renewal of a friendship stretching back to the 1780s (see Document 13). Madison and Monroe had worried together over the nation's Mississippi question, British debt repayments, and their own joint investment in Mohawk valley lands. Now it was apparent that Smith was disaffected from the administration, and that his brother could no longer practice any kind of political blackmail (see Document 13-a). Gallatin helped force the issue by offering his resignation, which Madison refused. He then wrote a conciliatory note to Monroe, received assurances that Monroe would be a loyal and trusting cabinet member, and the sorely needed revitalization of the cabinet took place. Smith left the cabinet in a huff, wrote his bitter pamphlet (see Note 2, Chapter 3), and disappeared into ignominy. Gallatin stayed on, his credentials with the president stronger than ever. Before the summer was over Rodney turned over the attorney general's office to the far more able William Pinkney, who had earned his spurs in the London legation and could be counted on to support Madison in any movement to smoke out English intentions. Eustis stayed on as secretary of war, and Paul Hamilton remained as secretary of the navy, but there was no doubt that the internal dissensions had at last been squelched. Madison was no longer afraid of Smith's or Giles's vengeance.

Although the Federalists taunted Madison as a man of bluster and no real substance, a president who talked tough but could not in reality be "kicked into a war," Madison had no intention of preparing for the 1812 presidential election by following his opponents' suggestions. With Monroe safely in the cabinet, Madison could assume that he would have no opposition of note from the South. What he needed to impress upon northern Republicans was not only his sincere desire for peace, but also his willingness to call for war. To this end he sent Monroe to hold talks with the newly arrived British minister, Augustus Foster. Admittedly, the proposition for Foster was the longest of long shots, but it was worth the gamble (see Document 13-c). If the British would give up the fiction of paper blockades (blockades by edict, not enforced by roving warships) and at the same time match the Duke of Cadore's letter with a similarly worded, vague announcement of the revocation of the Orders in Council—if England would do this—then the president would withdraw the Nonintercourse Act and reopen commerce with the two countries (see Document 13-d). "Two fake repeals would be considered to cancel each other out," as Perkins put it, and would allow Madison the appearance of having won a point by firmness.[5]

Had Foster grasped this hint and sent it to London for earnest consideration, the whole history of the next four years could have been different indeed. However, the British were in no mood to meet the United

States upon anything approaching equal terms. Arrogantly, Foster rejected Monroe's peace feelers and instead tried to exploit the administration's embarrassment over the Cadore letter by insisting that unless proof were furnished that the Berlin and Milan decrees had been revoked, the continuance of nonintercourse with England was absurd. Outwardly, all the signs of civility were shown to Foster, so that he almost had his head turned by the many courtesies administration figures showed the Englishman, but Madison was adamant. After Foster talked with the president he concluded that unless he could promise Madison that the Orders in Council might be repealed, "our discussions for the present at least were likely to be fruitless."[6] With Erskine's sad fall fresh in mind, however, Foster had no thought of making such a pledge.

## Mounting Pressures for War

Madison began to count the plusses and minuses in the situation and slowly came around to the position Gallatin had recommended to Jefferson almost three years earlier. In the last months of Jefferson's second term, when the failure of the embargo was evident to nearly everybody but Madison and Jefferson, Gallatin had then told the president he was not certain about whether to rely on economic coercion or outright war. "But I think that we must (or rather you must) decide the question absolutely, so that we may point out a decisive course either way to our friends."[7] By the summer of 1811, Madison's two trusted aides must have put the same proposition to the president. This was about the time his opposition claimed Madison was losing control in all directions. "The opinion is gaining ground rapidly that Mr. Madison will be impeached," the Baltimore *Federal Republican* gloated. Madison ignored such gossip as he tried to discern what was really in Foster's instructions. Had Foster come here to make trouble, or make peace, or neither? After a time Madison concluded it was probably the latter. "Foster seems more disposed to play the diplomatist, then the conciliatory negotiator," Madison observed (Madison to Monroe, July 2, 1811). The only way to find out was to keep probing (see Document 13-c).

Toward the end of July, Monroe tried to press Foster into action. He once again told Foster—this time officially—that if the Orders in Council were revoked and a real blockade set up, then "I am authorized to inform you [that this would] produce an immediate termination of the non-importation law, by an exercise of the power vested in the President for that purpose" (Monroe to Foster, July 23, 1811, Madison Papers). As late as October 1, 1811, Monroe was still hoping that something good could result from his talks with Foster. But he kept saying the same things in droning repetition, and Foster kept playing the dandy negotiator, willing to take months if necessary to settle a minor point.

And the means left for preventing an Anglo-American war were, in fact, almost exhausted. Madison had called a special session of Congress to convene in Washington on November 4, a month earlier than usual. A hint as to what was in Madison's mind came from the *National Intelligencer*, which was well-known as an administration vehicle through the editorship of the president's friend, Joseph Gales, Jr. Gales took over for Samuel H. Smith (now in poor health) and his paper warned that the president had been patient with England long enough. All the pressures for war were mounting, for after a year England was still ignoring the Cadore letter, and this made it clear that further self-control on the administration's part would only be interpreted as cowardice.[8]

The winds of change which blew Henry Clay into the House Speaker's chair also left the political barometer falling, insofar as the prospects for peace could be predicted. Clay was a new breed of politician, more clever than brainy, more deft than deep. He attempted to establish his own "ministry of all talents" by choosing committee chairmen who would follow his bidding (they did not, as it turned out). Crusty old Samuel Taggart, a Federalist fearful of what the hotheaded Republicans might do in the new Congress, looked about him in the House and thought he discerned four factions in the opposition: the War Hawks, who were somewhat stymied by a second faction opposed to all-out war, a third group (he labeled them "the scarecrows") which voted for war measures but were as hypocritical as saber-rattlers, and a fourth clique bent mainly on embarrassing Madison so as to oust him in the coming election.[9] Clay, Calhoun, and Felix Grundy were the leading Republicans, and they had sniffed the direction of public opinion—as practical politicians their instincts told them what to do. Madison, committed to presidential aloofness from congressional infighting, kept his innermost thoughts within his official family and allowed the vigorous congressmen to dominate the news. Before Congress assembled, the Republican newspapers began clamoring for a defiance of England and, if necessary, a declaration of war. Another Anglo-American naval clash, the continued Orders in Council, and Pinkney's recall from London left the War Hawks restless. Public opinion, except in New England, seemed prepared for a war. But was the president?

The answer was yes and no. In his third annual message to Congress, Madison urged the lawmakers to consider the "deep sense of the crisis in which you are assembled," and expressed extreme disappointment over England's reaction to the Cadore letter. Madison also gave France a few verbal slaps by calling attention to the unrestored American property seized under Napoleon's earlier edicts and to "the rigorous and unexpected restrictions to which their [American ships] trade with the French dominion has been subjected." Owing to both French and British restraints upon the United States, and their continued rejection of the claimed rights of a neutral America, Madison urged Congress to begin a program of military and naval preparedness (*Alternative 5*: see Document 13-e). Then, Madison inserted a sentence which Foster should have read with the greatest care. After alluding to the British cabinet's persistence in measures which "have the character as well as the effect of war on our lawful commerce," Madison added:

> With this evidence of hostile inflexibility in trampling on rights which
> no Independent Nation can relinquish; Congress will feel the duty of
> putting the United States into an armour and an attitude demanded by
> the crisis, and corresponding with the national spirit and expectations
> (see Document 13-e).

This was the plainest of talk, and showed that Madison was paying attention
to what the people in the West were saying, and to what the War Hawks in
Congress were hearing from their constituents. Although a cynical New
England congressman noted that the message was destined to sleep "quietly
in the Arms of the Committees to whom it has been sent," there were other
reactions on a different tack. Republican newspapers were enthusiastic about
the new tone of determination they discerned in the president, and the
bellwether Richmond *Enquirer* hinted that a new war for independence was
about to be fought. "In '76 we strove for our *existence*, as a nation; and now
we must strive for our *rights*, as one," the Republican journal warned.[10]

What many Americans did not realize was the extent to which the
republican president's patience had been justified. With or without the
embargo, British merchants were going through a bruising depression that
finally led to riots during the winter of 1810-1811, in the manufacturing
towns where unemployment was spreading at a time when food prices rose to
record heights. Warehouse shelves were groaning with unsold goods while
precious wheat, once bought cheaply and in vast quantities from America,
had to be smuggled in from Napoleon's Europe to meet the English demand.

During this time of distress, if anything could have aroused Parliament to
action, it was a business recession. When Parliament met in January, 1812,
the Prince Regent's opening remarks included a moderate allusion to
America, and the next day Prime Minister Perceval remarked that "England,
conscious of her own dignity, could bear more from America for peace's sake
than from any other Power on earth."[11] Pressure was building on all sides for
Parliament to revoke the Orders in Council and resume normal relations with
the United States, but at this critical juncture Pinkney was back at his home,
and a young relative of Robert Smith was the only American diplomat in
London for a time. Madison's message to Congress crossed the ocean,
meanwhile, and its more belligerent tone was added in the scales by those who
believed an American war would greatly worsen the economic difficulties
piling up in England.

Virtually none of this byplay in Parliament was known in America,
however. Young Smith was replaced by Jonathan Russell, shifted from Paris
in November, but his dispatches were not perceptive. Russell reported in
January that the Orders would not be relaxed unless "some great national
disaster" befell the government. When the voting in Parliament began to show
cracks in the heretofore rigid pro-Orders ranks, this good news was not rushed
to America by newspaper correspondents because there were none—and, of
course, there was no permanent cable until 1866. So the real thaw began to
take place while the Americans were becoming more determined than ever
that the time to fight was at hand. Most prophetically, the London *Globe* on

January 27, 1812, surmised that it was too late to avoid war. "The best friends of both countries consider the die as cast, and that sufficient time would not be allowed to avert the blow."[12] It is important to fix the dates of these pessimistic summaries, for in fact there was still time to prevent a war had the British cabinet taken the warnings seriously, or had the Madison administration been aware of the slow turnaround in thinking of an increasing number of members of Parliament. There is no need to waste time lamenting the absence of a cable, but there is some validity for historians to consider the lack of intelligence flowing across the Atlantic. Clearly, Russell lacked perception about the events taking place in London; otherwise he might have at the least reported some signs of a relaxed attitude owing to the business conditions and the general state of the British economy. Pinkney was a clever man and an able diplomat, and it is unthinkable that he would not have noticed a shift in the opinions of Britain's leading public men.

But, history is not based on "ifs." Events moved the timetable for war ahead, as the Battle of Tippecanoe proved.[13] Fought in November, 1811, as Madison's annual message was being read in New York, the battle cost the troops under William Henry Harrison a dear price, but the Indian village at Tippecanoe was destroyed (see Documents 14 and 14-a). When the news reached settlements and spread eastward, the newpapers proclaimed the skirmish a full-scale victory, and there was more than a hint that the Shawnee leaders (Tecumseh and his brother The Prophet) had been encouraged to challenge Governor Harrison by British agents. The press and the War Hawks hardly needed nudging, but Tippecanoe gave them a shove toward an even more warlike posture. Richard Mentor Johnson, a Kentucky congressman, had no hesitancy in blaming the battle on Indians "who were infuriated and made drunk by British traders." For five years America had stood insults from England with forbearance, but now it was time to substitute action for patience. "We must now oppose the further encroachments of Great Britain by war," shouted Johnson, "or formally annul the Declaration of Independence."[14]

## Notes

1. Bradford Perkins, *Prologue to War, England and the United States* (Berkeley: University of California Press, 1968), p. 259.

2. Henry Adams, *History of the Administration of Jefferson and Madison*, 9 vols. (Boston, 1891-96), vol. 5, p. 6.

3. Perkins, *Prologue to War*, p. 260.

4. Paul L. Ford, ed., *The Writings of Thomas Jefferson*, 10 vols. (New York, 1892-99), vol. 9, p. 324.

5. Perkins, *Prologue to War*, p. 281.

6. Irving Brant, *James Madison, the President, 1809-1812* (Indianapapolis: Bobbs Merrill, 1957), p. 343.

7. Quoted in Dumas Malone, *Jefferson the President, Second Term, 1805-1809* (Boston: Little, Brown & Co., 1974), p. 623.

8. Brant, *Madison, the President*, p. 355.

9. Perkins, *Prologue to War*, p. 346.

10.  Quoted in Perkins, *Prologue to War*, pp. 298-99.

11.  Adams, *History*, vol. 6, p. 271.

12.  Quoted in Perkins, *Prologue to War*, pp. 317, 325.

13.  Provoked by land-hungry Americans, the "battle" was a major effort to eliminate Indian resistance to the white man's treaties which were destroying the old colonial concept of a great Indian reservation separated from settlements by a neutral buffer zone.

14.  Adams, *History*, vol. 6, pp. 142-43.

# 5

# "Unleashing the Dogs of War"

The New Year came in with a blustering wind and more bad news from across the Atlantic. The French were still attacking American vessels, despite sanctimonious words from Cadore ("His Majesty loves the Americans"). Madison held a reception for the diplomatic corps, but used the occasion to lecture the French minister on his nation's duplicity.[1] The embarrassing truth was that the United States was inching toward war with England when the French also were showing no less regard for neutral rights. The War Hawks began to talk more about impressment than had been their practice, perhaps because that was almost the only factor tipping the balance in favor of an Anglo-American war if the nation had to fight someone to vindicate its own sense of honor (*Alternative 5*: see Document 14-a).

## Attempts to Prepare

What was Madison to do? Not much, for since he had given up all hope of peace there was nothing further that could be done except to write a war message to Congress. He conceived his duty in narrow limits, however; the burden now rested with Congress. On Capitol Hill, Congress appeared to be more cooperative than it had been in years, thanks to Speaker Clay and the War Hawks, but it was perhaps hard for a man of Madison's moral fiber to favor many of the programs that were the antithesis of Republican dogma—a large standing army, a deficit budget to support armaments, and a willingness to go to war when no foreign power was threatening invasion of American soil. Reluctant to levy new taxes, Congress hemmed and hawed for weeks until Gallatin suggested that new taxes might be necessary on whiskey among other items—along with an American version of a stamp act. Virtually no congressman was ready to deal with the impending deficit so candidly, so more talk and committee inaction allowed weeks to slide by without a concerted effort to prepare the nation for war, either economically or militarily. Proof of the latter came when a debate over the military bill revolved around a provision that volunteers to the new army were not to be sent into Canada or Spanish Florida without their own consent. The bill was passed and sent to the president in early February, but the matter of service beyond the nation's borders was unmentioned in the final version. A naval appropriations bill calling for $7,500,000 to pay for thirty-two men-of-war and frigates caused a soul-searching in the House that resulted in a fifty-nine to sixty-two defeat for the measure.

Faced now with a Congress that was talking war but voting for peace, Madison chose to shock the Congress and the nation with an exposé of British perfidy which, if proved true, showed that the English were hopeful of undermining the foundations of the Union. He knew nothing of the battle shaping in Parliament and wrote Jefferson that "all . . . we see from G. B. indicates an adherence to her mad policy toward the U. S." (Madison to Jefferson, Feb. 7, 1812). If it would take a bucket of ice water to wake up Congress and the nation, Madison had the next best thing. A packet of sensational letters was offered to Monroe that were purported to prove that the governor general of Canada had encouraged New Englanders to secede in the event of war. A French confidence man informed Monroe of the letters between Sir James Craig and one John Henry, who passed himself off as a British agent now prepared to switch allegiance (or information) for $75,000. The price was preposterous, but Monroe told Madison of the offer, and the president, all too eager to incriminate his Federalist critics around Boston, pushed the negotiations. Finally, for a sum of $50,000, the Frenchman turned over the packet of copied letters early in March. The letters were really rather tame stuff—much of what Henry copied could have been taken from columns of the *Columbian Centinel*—and it named no names, gave evidence of no specific plots, and had strings of asterisks that Henry claimed were used to protect his confidential sources (see Documents 14-b, 14-c, 14-d, 14-e, and 14-f).

In short, Madison and Monroe had been taken in much like a pair of country rubes, and paid $50,000 from the treasury in the bad bargain—"only $2,500 less than the entire cost of the *U. S. S. Hornet*."[2] It would have been to Madison's credit if he had taken the letters, tied them in a bundle with a secret seal, and shipped them back to the State Department with orders to store them in a dark, dark corner. But Madison's zeal to expose the last real holdouts against an Anglo-American war, the Boston Federalists, overcame his good judgment. Whatever the shortcomings of the Henry letters, they at least appeared to prove that a British spy had been operating in New England—and doubtless Madison was prepared to let the public mind fill in the details after Congress read the shocking news. This seems to have been in Madison's mind (there is hardly any other explanation), and so he sent the letters to Congress on March 9. A British spy had intrigued with disaffected Americans in Boston, and a plot had been uncovered whereby the Union would be destroyed and "the eastern part thereof [would form] into a political connexion with Great Britain" (see Document 14-e). By this petty act, Madison revealed a weakness that seems inconsistent in his character. Personally honest and inclined toward magnanimity, Madison's conduct in the Henry letters affair was blundering and bound to boomerang. As Morison pointed out, the eager acceptance of the letters (he had not seen their contents before the money was paid) showed Madison to be gullible, and the use of $50,000 for such a partisan purpose by a man of proclaimed frugality raised a question of political morality.

The Henry letters caused a momentary sensation. Congress became worked up and demanded an investigation, and then the matter was dropped when it seemed to have backfired. By the end of March, Madison heard from a kinsman who served in Congress that Federalist newspaper comments on the Henry letters teemed with "animadversions . . . [which] proves that Great Britain with much justice counts upon a party amongst us. War alone can furnish a remedy for this deplorable malady in the body politic" (see Document 14-g). However, proof that the letters were not needed to push Congress into a more forthright position had come several days before Madison had sent the packet to Capitol Hill, when a tax bill passed handily to provide the money needed for the impending struggle. "The H. of Rs. have got down the dose of taxes," he reported to Jefferson. "It is the strongest proof they could give that they do not mean to flinch from the contest to which the mad conduct of G. B. drives them" (Madison to Jefferson, March 6, 1812). Too good a friend to look into the Henry business closely, Jefferson replied that the exposé "will prove to the people of England, beyond the power of palliation by the ministry[,] that the war is caused by the wrongs of their own nation" (Jefferson to Madison, March 26, 1912; see Documents 14-h and 14-k).

Even from his remote base at Monticello, Jefferson could see that war was all but an accomplished fact (*Alternative 5*: see Document 14-j). The last step needed before the public in all sections would be ready for the war message to Congress was, fittingly, a dramatic sea voyage by the *U.S.S. Hornet* (see Document 14-i). In truth, the awaited arrival of the warship was dramatic only in that the administration used every means to make the voyage appear to be a last effort to keep "from unleashing the dogs of war." A Kentucky editor felt the pressure across the mountains: "Ever since her sailing the cant word has been, the *Hornet*, the *Hornet*—what a sting she will bring on her return!!"[3] No word came, so Congress extended the embargo against England for another ninety days, and Madison wondered what had kept the *Hornet* so long at sea. "The delay of the Hornet is inexplicable," he told Jefferson (Madison to Jefferson, April 3, 1812). Meanwhile, Congress openly discussed war as a certainty, and some War Hawks wondered how many weeks it would take to invade and conquer Canada. In New York, the Federalist *Evening Post*, trying to fling logic into the balance against war, warned that if Americans were going to fight England for "pecuniary redress . . . the measure is perfect madness. You will lose millions when you will gain a cent. The expense will be enormous. It will ruin our country." The Louisiana Purchase had already wasted $15 million. "And will you spend thousands of million in conquering a province which, were it made a present to us, would not be worth accepting? Our territories are already too large. The desire to annex Canada . . . is as base an ambition as ever burned in the bosom of Alexander" (New York *Evening Post*, April 21, 1812).[4]

## Getting Congressional Support

Since the beginning of 1812 everything had turned topsyturvy for the Federalists. As Henry Adams saw it, "they seemed to lose reason" as their strategy switched from plain obstructionism to complicity in Madison's showdown policy on the ground that a war would destroy the Republican party. The congressional Federalists confessed to the British minister in private that if a war vote came they would support Madison, convinced "that war will turn out the Administration, and then they will have their own way, and make a solid peace with Great Britain."[5] There was no accounting for what might happen to Madison's program in such circumstances, for every member of Congress at times seemed to think he was a party unto himself.

In spite of the public anticipation of some surprising news on the arrival of the *Hornet*, Madison's mind had been made up for some time (see Document 15). Any evidence that Napoleon was living up to his promises would have brought a hurried war message to Congress, but instead the trickle of news indicated more depredations by the French navy. Congress debated a ninety-day embargo that was meant to stop further losses at sea and clear the decks for a war with England, as Monroe hinted to the French minister. Plainspoken congressional supporters of the bill claimed that its passage was a preliminary to war, and on that ground it had passed. Now the watchful waiting for the *Hornet* added to the drama of the moment, and the only message that could reverse the trend of events begun on November 4, 1811, with the special session would have been a startling announcement that England had revoked the Orders in Council. Of course, Madison expected no such news, but he was now a victim of his own propaganda, for the *National Intelligencer* and other Republican journals had repeatedly indicated that momentous events hinged upon the dispatches aboard the *Hornet*.

*Hornet* or no *Hornet*, the presidential election loomed and Congress needed to act before spring. On May 18, the usual device for nominating a president—the congressional caucus—met and with little fanfare renominated Madison. In a bow to surly New England, Elbridge Gerry was chosen for the vice-president's post, since George Clinton had died in that office only a few weeks earlier. New York Republicans quickly switched their allegiance to Clinton's kinsman, Dewitt Clinton, and voted to cast their votes for the challenger of Madison's reelection bid. The news of political jockeying was somewhat muted, however, by the arrival in New York harbor on May 19 of the *Hornet*. Official papers on the warship were sped by express southward and, if the newspapers are to be believed, the nation held its breath for a sign from Washington. Was it peace or war?

For a few days the situation was confused as the rumors indicated that all expectations of some friendly signs from either France or England were baseless. "The 'Hornet' has at last arrived," the French minister reported. "On the rumor of this news, the avenues of the State Department were thronged by a crowd of members of both Houses of Congress, as well as by strangers and citizens, impatient to know what this long-expected vessel had brought. Soon it was learned that the 'Hornet' had brought nothing favorable. . . . On this news, the furious declamations of the Federalists . . . were redoubled; the Republicans, deceived in their hopes, joined in the outcry, and for three days nothing was heard but a general cry for war against France and England at once" (Seurier to Maret, May 27, 1812).[6]

As Perkins has shown, there was still a final escape hatch left open for Madison, had he chosen to use it. The English army fighting in Spain was provisioned largely with American foodstuffs. Grain shipments from the United States to the Peninsula had leaped from 230,000 bushels in 1810 to 835,000 in 1811. Diplomats who were aware of this chink in the English armor had suggested that Madison might close this trade and force England to offer a quid pro quo with the Orders in Council. Madison decided not to press the matter, however, and under the nonimportation laws exports to feed the British army flowed through eastern ports until almost the moment war was declared.[7]

Perhaps it was fortunate for Madison that the device of polling public opinion was unknown at this stage, for much of the evidence indicates that if anything, the country was about evenly divided on the necessity of war once the disappointment of the *Hornet's* dispatches had worn off. There had been some talk in the early spring of a recess by Congress to let the air clear. Madison plainly was bewildered, for he knew what he thought should be done, but he was not sure that Congress would swallow the pill of a declaration of war against England. He wrote Jefferson that "the business is become more than ever puzzling. To go to war with Engd. and not with France arms the federalists with new matter, and divides the Republicans. . . . To go to war agst both, presents a thousand difficulties; above all that of shutting all the ports of the Continent of Europe agst. our Cruisers who can do little without the use of them." There was some talk of a "triangular war as it is called,·' on the ground that it might force one of the European powers to negotiate a peace promptly. "But even this advantage is not certain," Madison confessed (*Alternative 5*: see Document 14-k).

Madison waited for some signal that Congress would back him in a war message. The question was not so much of timing but of votes for a further delay would mean that the embargo would expire, and the whole question would come up again, possibly with an embarrassing outcome for the administration. Thus it appeared that it might be easier to declare war than to go through the motions of imposing still another embargo. No doubt to Madison's considerable relief Speaker Clay joined with several other War Hawks and they took the long ride down Pennsylvania Avenue to assure the president that if he asked for war they would find the votes to pass the declaration. This was all the assurance Madison needed [9]

## War Declared

Madison thus decided to commit the nation to a war which Monroe favored, Gallatin opposed, and Pinkney thought premature. Only the pledges from Clay's delegation tipped the balance for war, for Madison until then had "feared that Congress would either be unable or unwilling to provide him with the necessary supplies of money and men, to carry it on to a successful issue."[9] Moreover, the kind of war Madison was asking the country to leap into was not Napoleon's kind of war—it was to be a short, almost bloodless war, lasting perhaps nine months—a "hot" war to end all the confusion of a "cold" one, and to prove that the United States was willing to risk blook and treasure for its expanding commercial interests in overseas commodity markets.

In his war message of June 1, 1812, Madison recounted all the old grievances: impressment, the seizure of ships and cargoes, British warships sailing into American harbors for belligerent acts, and naval blockades that strangled maritime and agricultural pursuits. The refusal of England to recognize that France had revoked her decrees, and her persistence in the Orders in Council while granting to the British traders a means of "supplying the wants of her enemies" was a cynical effort to expand English markets at American expense. "She carries on a war against the lawful commerce of a friend that she may the better carry on a commerce with an enemy," Madison said, repeating an old charge. He recalled the abortive negotiations with Erskine (without mentioning his name) and noted that the whole affair "was disavowed by the British Government without any explanations which could at that time repress the belief that the disavowal proceeded from a spirit of hostility to the commercial rights and prosperity of the United States." There was more talk of Indian atrocities on the frontier that appeared to have been encouraged by the British, of "our seafaring citizens still the daily victims of lawless violence," and other circumstances that made it plain there was an undeclared war against the United States being waged by England at that moment.

Thus for the bill of particulars, Madison concluded, as he brought his indictment of England to an end. Whether the nation would follow a passive course or throw force against force was "a solemn question which the Constitution wisely confides to the legislative department of the Government." Madison still had a parting shot for France. He had presented Congress with "a solemn alternative" regarding England, but was not so positive about what to do about France. Her obnoxious decrees had been revoked but the French still were seizing ships and men, and yet "no indemnity had been provided or satisfactorily pledged for the extensive spoliations committed." However, the door was not closed, and he hinted that the pending discussions in Paris might conclude favorably, although—again—it would be up to Congress to decide "on the course due to the rights, the interests, and the honor of our country" (*Alternative 5*: see Document 15).

Clay delivered on his promise, and the United States was soon involved in its second war for independence and its first war as a polarized nation. The war vote went along sectional lines; the North generally opposed the declaration, while the South and West favored it. Obviously, the frontiersmen and planters had voted the country into a war that mainly would be fought by seamen from northern ports.

Of course, Madison could not foresee the internal animosity that lay ahead. He signed the declaration of war on June 19, and thereby admitted that the policy he had helped establish eight years earlier had been a failure. This peaceable man believed that the only alternative left had been submission and humiliation; and he asked for the blessing of Divine Providence as the United States trooped to war. When the news of the revoked Orders in Council came that summer the American war machine was not in gear, but the nation was already too committed for any sudden reversal of its decision.

Hindsight offers harsh judgments on men and their motives. If Madison and his aides could have exercised saintly patience for perhaps another year, war with England probably could have been averted. But the problem was of long standing, and in early 1812 no one could have predicted the May 11 assassination of Perceval, the change in Parliament's attitude toward the Orders following the prime minister's murder, or the demise of Napoleon within three years. Indeed, Napoleon had been a conspicuous world figure for nearly twenty years and gave every promise of being one for perhaps another twenty (he was only forty-three when Madison abandoned his peace efforts). At the time, it seemed to Madison that the United States would be buffeted between the two contending powers for as far into the future as any prudent man could see. The large naval expenditures that would have given sinews to American protests were anathema to Madison as a political gesture (since the Federalists had long favored a large navy), as a waste of public money, and as a contradiction to republican principles.[10] And finally, Madison had no desire to be remembered as the president who helped found the United States, only to allow his country to fall short of her aspirations for an independent existence in the family of nations. After a long search for another solution, Madison came to see that the only alternatives were a humiliated, enfeebled American republic or a war. Reluctantly, but with resolution, peace-loving James Madison chose war.

## Notes

1.  Ralph Ketcham, *James Madison* (New York: Macmillan Co., 1971), p. 514.
2.  Samuel E. Morison, *By Land and by Sea* (New York: 1953), p. 272.
3.  Quoted in Bradford Perkins, *Prologue to War, England and the United States* (Berkeley: University of California Press, 1968), p. 376.
4.  Quoted in Allan Nevins, *American Press Opinion, Washington to Coolidge* (New York: D. C. Heath & Company, 1928), p. 48.
5.  Henry Adams, *History of the Administration of Jefferson and Madison*, 9 vols. (Boston, 1891-96), vol. 6, p. 172.
6.  Quoted in Adams, *History*, vol. 6, p. 217.
7.  Perkins, *Prologue to War*, p. 382.

8. Gaillard Hunt, "Joseph Gales on the War Manifesto of 1812," *American Historical Review* 13 (1907-1908): 309.

9. John Quincy Adams, *The Lives of James Madison and James Monroe* (Buffalo, 1850), p. 173.

10. One historian who rejects the theory that economic factors brought on the war is Norman K. Risjord, "1812: Conservatives, War Hawks, and the Nation's Honor," *William and Mary Quarterly*, 3rd. ser., 18 (1961): 196-7.

# Part two

# Documents of the Decision

# A Note on the Documents

In history, as in other human activities, many things may change over the years but there is one constant: a belief that the truth of a proposition lies in the original materials created by the circumstances. This fundamental tenet in historiography became the preachment of the German historians in the nineteenth century, who trained a generation of Americans that would return to this country and spread the gospel of the document. Over a century later, we are still convinced that one of the values of history, in all times, is the opportunity presented by research in the materials for each generation to make its own assessment of the truth. Postulating basic honesty, the earnest student can take many roads to arrive at the final summary, and the humble scholar will realize that his judgment is tentative—that *the definitive word can never be said*. But each generation owes it to itself to make a search for "a concept of human reality at a given moment in history" i.e., the truth.*

The documents printed here should lead into a study of the personality of James Madison as a congressman of pacific disposition whom fate cast in the role of a war president. How this irony is produced by the vicissitudes of political life should become apparent as the reader proceeds from the visionary ideas of a forty-year-old congressman to the official messages of a somewhat embittered, disillusioned old president. In all that James Madison did there was always one justification—he loved the Union more than life itself.

*For this splendid definition of truth the author is indebted to Professor Curtis P. Nettels of Cornell University.

# 1

# Madison's Views on Peace and War While in Congress, 1792

Madison quickly emerged in the First Congress (1789) as a leading exponent of the political philosophy now associated with the republicanism of Jefferson and his circle. No tenent in that philosophy was as fixed as the idea that since "the earth belongs to the living," wars which create huge debts should be avoided at all costs, not so much for the human misery they generate as for the unfair burden their costs impose on distant generations. In this anonymous newspaper essay, Madison advanced an idea for "Universal Peace" which brimmed with republicanism; had Madison still felt this way twenty years later, perhaps he would have been more eager to turn the other cheek.

## Document†

### UNIVERSAL PEACE

Among the various reforms which have been offered to the world, the projects for universal peace have done the greatest honor to the hearts, though they seem to have done very little to the heads, of their authors.

Rousseau, the most distinguished of these philanthropists, has recommended a confederation of sovereigns, under a council of deputies, for the double purpose of arbitrating external controversies among nations, and of guarantying their respective governments against internal revolutions. He was aware neither of the impossibility of executing his pacific plan among governments which feel so many allurements to war, nor, what is more extraordinary, of the tendency of his plan to perpetuate arbitrary power wherever it existed; and, by extinguishing the hope of one day seeing an end of oppression, to cut off the only source of consolation remaining to the oppressed.

A universal and perpetual peace, it is to be feared, is in the catalogue of events which will never exist but in the imaginations of visionary philosophers, or in the breasts of benevolent enthusiasts. It is still, however, true, that war contains so much folly, as well as wickedness, that much is to

†From: Philadelphia *National Gazette*, February 2, 1792.

be hoped from the progress of reason; and if anything is to be hoped, everything ought to be tried.

Wars may be divided into two classes: one flowing from the mere will of the government; the other according with the will of the society itself.

Those of the first class can no otherwise be prevented than by such a reformation of the government as may identify its will with the will of the society. The project of Rousseau was, consequently, as preposterous as it was impotent. Instead of beginning with an external application, and even precluding internal remedies, he ought to have commenced with, and chiefly relied on, the latter prescription.

He should have said, whilst war is to depend on those whose ambition, whose revenge, whose avidity, or whose caprice may contradict the sentiment of community, and yet be controlled by it; whilst war is to be declared by those who are to spend the public money, not by those who are to pay it; by those who are to direct the public forces, not by those who are to support them; by those whose power is to be raised, not by those whose chains may be riveted, the disease must continue to be *hereditary* like the government of which it is the offspring. As the first step towards a cure, the government itself must be regenerated. Its will must be made subordinate to, or rather the same with, the will of the community.

Had Rousseau lived to see the Constitutions of the United States and of France, his judgment might have escaped the censure to which his project has exposed it.

The other class of wars, corresponding with the public will, are less susceptible of remedy.

There are antidotes, nevertheless, which may not be without their efficacy. As wars of the first class were to be prevented by subjecting the will of the government to the will of the society, those of the second can only be controlled by subjecting the will of the society to the reason of the society; by establishing permanent and constitutional maxims of conduct, which may prevail over occasional impressions, and inconsiderate pursuits.

Here our republican philosopher might have proposed as a model to lawgivers, that war should not only be declared by the authority of the people, whose toils and treasures are to support its burdens, instead of the government which is to reap its fruits; but that each generation should be made to bear the burden of its own wars, instead of carrying them on at the expense of other generations. And to give the fullest energy to his plan, he might have added, that each generation should not only bear its own burdens, but that the taxes composing them should include a due proportion of such as by their direct operation keep the people awake, along with those which, being wrapped up in other payments, may leave them asleep, to misapplications of their money.

To the objection, if started, that where the benefits of war descend to succeeding generations, the burdens ought also to descend, he might have answered, that the exceptions could not be easily made; that, if attempted, they must be made by one only of the parties interested; that in the alternative of sacrificing exceptions to general rules, or of converting exceptions into general rules, the former is the lesser evil; that the expense of *necessary* wars will never exceed the resources of an *entire* generation; that, in fine, the objection vanishes before the *fact* that in every nation which has drawn on posterity for the support of its wars, *the accumulated interest* of its perpetual debts has soon become more than a *sufficient principal* for all its exigencies.

Were a nation to impose such restraints on itself, avarice would be sure to calculate the expenses of ambition; in the equipoise of these passions, reason would be free to decide for the public good, and an ample reward accrue to the State—first, from the avoidance of all its wars of folly; secondly, from the vigor of its unwasted resources for wars of necessity and defence. Were all nations to follow the example, the reward would be doubled to each, and the temple of Janus might be shut, never to be opened more.

Had Rousseau lived to see the rapid progress of reason and reformation, which the present day exhibits, the philanthropy which dictated his project would find a rich enjoyment in the scene before him; and after tracing the past frequency of wars to a will in the government independent of the will of the people, to the practice by each generation of taxing the principal of its debts on future generations, and to the facility with which each generation is seduced into assumptions of the interest, by the deceptive species of taxes which pay it, he would contemplate in a reform of every government subjecting its will to that of the people, in a subjection of each generation to the payment of its own debts, and in a substitution of a more palpable, in place of an imperceptible mode of paying them, the only hope of UNIVERSAL AND PERPETUAL PEACE.

# 2

# Monroe Urges a Threat of War

Monroe had been sent to London as the American minister to the Court of Saint James. He went to Madrid in an effort to negotiate differences between the United States on boundaries, spoliations claims, and other matters but soon found that there was no reason to expect the mission would succeed. He returned to London in May, 1805, on the day when the *Essex* case was decided by a British admiralty court, which held that the so-called broken voyage in neutral trade, allowed since the Jay Treaty, was now illegal. In practical terms the decision hit American shipping a reeling blow, for it meant that a United States ship could not load at a French West Indian port, drop anchor at an American harbor for new papers, and then proceed to London without being subject to British seizure and condemnation. Monroe had intended to quit London and return to America, but he now delayed his plans in order to lodge a protest with the British Foreign Office.

This anguished letter from Monroe to Madison shows that not all Republicans were inclined to turn the other cheek when caught between the fire of a British cruiser or a Spanish man-of-war. The latter fleet was soon out of commission, for Nelson defeated the combined French-Spanish armada at Trafalgar a few days after the letter was written. But Madison knew from this letter that there was a mounting spirit of anger that would have to be reckoned with, despite his and the president's belief that a vigilant republic could steer safely through the war lanes.

Surely Madison and Jefferson discussed Monroe's letter, although they were probably either amused or horrified at his specific suggestions of running the risks of a triangular war with England, Spain, and the United States. Instead, they looked toward commercial restrictions and economic coercion as the sensible, republican answer to America's woes.

*Document 2-a†*

## Monroe to Secretary of State Madison

London October 18, 1805.

Sir

I sent you lately by Col. Mercer my note to Lord Mulgrave of the 23. ulto. relative to the late seizure of our vessels, in which I thought proper to advert, at the conclusion, to the other topicks that were depending when I left this country for Spain. I endeavoured to touch those topicks, especially the insults in our ports and the impressment of our seamen, in a manner to shew a due sensibility to such outrages, and if possible to conciliate this government to concur in a suitable arrangement to prevent the like in future. It seemed to be improper and it was certainly useless to touch them without expressing the sense which the President entertained of the injury and indignity to which the United States had thereby been exposed. The acts were of a nature to require it, and the conduct of this government since had increased the obligation to do it. It appeared also by your letters, which were received by Mr. Purviance in my absence, that the President expected that this government [Great Britain] would make such an example of the officers who had most signalized themselves, by their misconduct, as would serve as a warning to the commanders of other vessels, who may hereafter seek shelter or hospitality in our ports. This had not been done. On the contrary, I was informed, by the best authority, that Captain Bradley of the Cambrian, whose conduct had been most offensive, had been promoted immediately on his return to the command of a ship of the line. . . . Under such circumstances it seemed to be impossible to separate the officer from the government in those outrages, and quite useless to demand the censure of him. I thought it therefore most adviseable in the present stage at least, to treat the affair in a general way, rather than in reference to a particular occurrence, and in looking to the offensive object, and paying any regard to what was due to the U. States, the manner was as conciliating as I could make it. . . .

I have no doubt that the seizure of our vessels was a deliberate act of this government. I do not know that the measure was regularly submitted to and decided in the Cabinet, but I am satisfied that that department of it having cognizance of and controul over the business dictated the measure. The circumstances attending the transaction justify this opinion. Before the coalition with Russia and Sweden the commerce was free. The blow was given when that coalition was formed. G. Britain has shewn much political arrangement in the whole of this affair. By the amendatory article of her treaty with Russia in 1801, the latter abandons the right to the direct trade between the colonies of an enemy and the parent country, and agrees to rest on the ground which the U. States might hold in that respect. It is to be presumed that she declined the seizure before the coalition was formed with

†From: Monroe Papers, Library of Congress, Washington, D.C.

the Northern powers lest it might alarm them and endanger the coalition; and that she made the seizure afterwards on the idea that as they were embarked in the war with her, they would become indifferent to the object and leave her free to push her pretentions against us. The manner in which the pressure is made, being thro' the Admiralty Court, on a pretext that the trade is direct, altho' the articles were landed in our ports and the duties paid on them, is equally a proof of management on her part. It was obviously intended to urge, indeed Lord Mulgrave in our first interview, began by urging, that there had been no new measure, that the government had not acted in the business, while the Court by considering every species of that commerce, direct, and every accommodation on the part of our citizens with previous regulations fraudulent and evasive, should push the pretentions of the government to such an extent as to annihilate it altogether. Lord Mulgrave insisted in express terms, in the second interview, that we ought not to carry it on at all with the parent Country; that the importation into our country ought to be confined to the supplies necessary for the home consumption. I am equally confident that if G. Britain should succeed in establishing her pretentions against us, she would avail herself of the example hereafter with the Northern Powers. It is therefore a question of great importance to them also

With respect to our other concerns with G. Britain I am sorry to say that I do not see any prospect of arranging them on just and reasonable terms at the present time. No disposition has been shewn to prescribe by treaty any restraint on the impressment of our seamen, whenever the government may be so disposed, or even when any of it's officers in the West Indies or elsewhere may think fit. On the subject of boundary nothing has been lately said, nor does there appear to be any inclination to enter on it. I have also reason to think that this government is equally disposed to postpone an arrangement of our commerce in general, by treaty, for any number of years. On this point however I cannot speak with so much confidence as on the others, having never made any proposition, which was calculated to obtain an explicit declaration of its sentiments. The conversations which I had with Lords Hawkesbury and Harrowby before I went to Spain on the other subjects, naturally brought this into view, but being incidentally it was only slightly touched. The proposition which was made by the latter to consider the treaty of 1794 in force, was as a temporary expedient, not a permanent regulation. From that circumstance and the manner in which they both spoke of that treaty, I concluded that their government would be willing to revive it, for an equal term. It might however have been made only to obtain delay. You will observe that in my note of the 23. ulto. I have taken the liberty to mention the subject, in a manner to shew that it is not one to which the U. States are indifferent, or which the President wishes to postpone. Altho' I have no power to form a treaty, of so comprehensive a nature, yet I thought I might with propriety open the subject, so far at least as to ascertain the views of this government on it, for your information.

On a review of the conduct of this government towards the United States, from the commencement of the war, I am inclined to think that the delay which has been so studiously sought in all these concerns is the part of a system, and that it is intended as circumstances favor, to subject our commerce at present and hereafter to every restraint in their power. It is certain that the greatest jealousy is entertained of our present and increasing prosperity, and I am satisfied that nothing which is likely to succeed, will be left untried to impair it. That this sentiment has taken a deep hold of the publick councils here, was sufficiently proved by the late seizures, being at a time when the state of our affairs with Spain menac'd a rupture, from which G. Britain could not fail to derive the most solid advantages. It was natural to expect, especially when we advert to the then critical situation of this country, that the government would have seized the opportunity to promote that tendency by a more just and enlightened policy. The part however which it acted was calculated, so far as depended on it, to prevent one. It proved satisfactorily that no event is deemed more unfavorable to G. Britain than the growing importance of the U. States and that it is a primary object of her government to check if not to crush it. It is possible that this government may be influenced in its conduct, by a belief that the U. States will not revive the treaty of 1794, unless they be driven to it by such means. It may also be attributable to a policy still more unfriendly. There is cause to believe that many prejudices are still fostered here, in certain circles at least, which the experience of multiplied and striking facts ought long since to have swept away. Among them it is proper to mention an opinion which many do not hesitate to avow, that the U. States are by the nature of their government, being popular, incapable of any great, vigorous or persevering exertion: that they cannot for example resist a system of commercial hostility from this country, but must yield to the pressure. It is useless to mention other prejudices still more idle, which had influence on past measures and certainly still exist with many of great consideration. With such a view of their interest, of the means of promoting it, and the confidence which is entertained of success, it cannot be doubted that it is their intention to push their fortune in every practicable line at our expence. The late seizure is probably an experiment, on this principle, of what the U. States will bear, and the delay which is observed in answering my letters only an expedient to give the government time to see its effect. If it succeeds they will I presume pursue the advantage gained to the greatest extent in all the relations subsisting between the two countries, more especially in the impressment of our seamen, the prostration and pillage of our commerce thro' the war, and in the more elevated tone of the government in a future negotiation. If it fails I am equally confident that their whole system of conduct towards the U. States will change, and that it will then be easy to adjust our affairs with this country, and place them on an equal, and reciprocally advantageous footing. Perhaps no time was ever more favorable for resisting these unjust encroachments than the present one. The conduct of our government is universally known to have been just, friendly, and conciliating towards G. Britain, while the attack by her government on the U. States is as universally known to be unjust, wanton & unprovoked. The measure has wounded deeply the interests of many of her own people and is not a popular one. The U. States furnish them at all times one of the best markets for their manufactures, and at present almost the only one. Her colonies are dependant on us. Harrassed as they already are with the war, and the menaces of a powerful adversary, a state of hostility with us, would probably go far to throw this country into confusion. It is an event which the ministry would find it difficult, and therefore cannot I presume be willing to encounter.

But is it safe for the U. States to attempt a vindication of their rights and interests in a decisive manner, with Spain and Britain at the same time? Will it not unite them against us and otherwise do us most essential injury? This is certainly a very important consideration and will of course be maturely weighed by our government. In my view of the subject the cases do not interfere. We probably never shall be able to settle our concerns with either power, without pushing our just claims on each with the greatest decision. At present, tho' at war with each other they harmonize in a system of aggression against us, as far as it is possible in such a state. Is it not presumeable then that at peace their harmony will be greater and its effect more injurious? It seems to be a question simply whether we will resist their unjust pressure at this time or defer it to some other opportunity, and surely none can be more favorable for us or less so for them. They are now respectively much in our power. We can wound both essentially, should it be necessary to push things to that extremity, without receiving much comparative injury in return. I am strong in the opinion that a pressure on each at the same time would produce a good effect with the other. Success with either could not well fail to produce it with the other. I am far from thinking that the incident with Britain should change our conduct towards Spain, or that the necessity we may be under to push our pretentions with Spain should relax our exertions against Britain. Some considerations indeed occur which make it probable that the latter incident was a fortunate one. By pressing both at the same time France may find herself relieved from a dilemma, in which a pressure on Spain alone, might place her, in consideration of her conduct in the late negotiation; and being desirous to encourage our misunderstanding with England she may be prompted to promote an adjustment of our differences with Spain, to leave us free to push the object with England. As these subjects have been practically much under my view in the trusts with which I have been honored by the President, and have entirely engrossed my attention I have thought that it would be agreeable to you to receive the result of my relfections on them. I am, Sir, with great respect & esteem,

### Document 2-b†

The letter from Christopher Gore to Madison sets forth the kind of depredation the British navy was inflicting on American commerce. The irony of the *Indus* seizure was that Gore was a leading Federalist who would ride into the Massachusetts governor's mansion in the reaction to the Republican program of restricted maritime trade.

Christopher Gore to Madison

Boston, *November* 18, 1805.

SIR:

The ship Indus, David Myrick, master, was taken by His Britannic Majesty's ship the Cambrian, Captain John P. Beresford, in latitude thirty-one degrees thirty minutes north, and longitude sixty-one degrees fifty-six minutes west, and sent to Halifax, where she, and all the property on board, belonging to the owners, master, and supercargo, were condemned, on the ground, as is said, of the illegality of the trade which she was prosecuting at the time of the capture. . . . The voyage which the Indus was performing, when captured, was direct from Batavia to Boston, there to terminate. A trade perfectly ⸲ legal, not only in the understanding of the owners, but so acknowledged, admitted, and declared by Great Britain, in her practice, for ten years past, in her instructions to her cruisers, in the decrees of her courts, and in the rules and principles advanced by her judges in promulgating their decrees.

The principle understood to be assumed by Great Britain is, that, in time of war, a trade carried on between two independent nations, one neutral and the other belligerent, is unlawful in the neutral, if the same trade was not allowed and practised in time of peace. This principle, though assumed by Great Britain, is now, and always has been, resisted as unsound, by every other nation. She always assumes as a fact, that the trade with a colony has always been confined, exclusively, to ships of the parent country. In virtue, therefore, of this assumption of principle and fact, she deems unlawful and derogatory to her rights, the trade of a neutral with the colonies of her enemies. . . .

This principle was first brought forward in the war of 1756, and was then attempted to be supported on the doctrinces advanced by Bynkershock. You, sir, to whom the writings of this eminent civilian are doubtless familiar, must be aware, that the rule laid down by him is brought forward to a very different purpose; and from the manner in which he treats on the rights of neutrals, and the historical fact quoted from Livy to illustrate and sanction the principle asserted, shows that it can by no means warrant the proceedings which it has been attempted to justify; and that there is no analogy between the case cited and that of the mere peaceable trade of a neutral with a belligerent, in articles not contraband of war, nor to places under blockade. . . .

Great Britain acts upon this principle: at one time she executes her

†From: *American State Papers: Foreign Relations*, vol. 2, pp. 756-59.

navigation law with strictness; at other times she relaxes most of its regulations, according to the estimate she forms of advantage or disadvantage to be derived from its execution or relaxation; neither does she allow the competence of any foreign Power to call in question her right to do so. In time of peace she compels a strict adherence to the principles and letter of her navigation act: in time of war she suspends most of its provisions, and to this she is doubtless induced by the paramount interest of manning her navy, whereby she is enabled to employ a much greater number of seamen in her own defence, and to destroy the commerce of her foes. . . .

If this new and extraordinary doctrine of continuity is maintained on the part of Great Britain, and acquiesced in by the United States, a very large property, now afloat, may be subject to condemnation, and it must follow that an extensive trade, which has been carried on with great advantage by the United States for these twelve years, and admitted to be lawful, will be totally annihilated.

The Indus and cargo have been condemned on the mere possibility that the same might go to Europe from Boston in case of peace, in which event Great Britain could pretend to no authority to question the voyage she should make.

Now, to adopt a principle of dubious right in its own nature, and then to extend such principle to a further restriction of the trade of the neutral, without notice, is spreading a snare to entrap the property and defeat the acknowledged rights to which he is entitled. . . . In the present case they [the owners] considered that, according to the clearest evidence of those rules [of British courts on the rights of neutrals], they incurred no risk from British cruisers. . . .

# 3

# Madison's Pamphlet Answer to England, 1806

The richest exchange in American history may have been the conversations between Jefferson and Madison that went on in the White House from March 1801 to March 1809. But unluckily for historians, there is scant record of this harmonious relationship since the notes (if made) are missing, and the two Republicans were too busy to return from their business chores to write memoirs of the day's events. Perhaps Madison had learned his lesson at the Federal Convention and had no intention of writing dispatches all day and memoirs all night.

Madison found time to do some writing, however, on a subject often discussed with Jefferson—the illegality of British seizures of neutral commerce. The broken-voyage concept, overruled in the *Essex* case, had turned the British navy loose on American commerce, and the scholar in Madison led him to compile a lengthy treatise which he titled *Examination of the British Doctrine, which subjects to capture a Neutral Trade Not Open in Time of Peace*. Published anonymously at about the time James Stephen's anti-American *War in Disguise; or, the Frauds of the Neutral Flags* appeared in London, Madison's long tract was a direct attack on the British Rule of 1756, which was reimposed by the *Essex* decision in May, 1805. Madison wrote nearly seventy thousand words in defense of the American right to trade with the colonies of England's enemies while "she trades herself with her enemies, and invites them to trade with her colonies." Jefferson had used much the same language in his annual message the previous December, and now the secretary of state was going before the court of world opinion to show that England was standing firm on an illegal doctrine that had "as its *true foundation a mere superiority of force.*"

*Document 3-a†*

### Madison to James Monroe

Department of State
Dear Sir,                                                                       January 13th, 1806
The perseverance of the British Government in the principle which licenses

†From: U. S., Department of State Diplomatic Instruction Series, National Archives, Washington, D. C.

the depredations on our commerce in Colonial productions, with the losses already sustained and still apprehended by our merchants, has produced a very general indignation throughout this Country, and mak[es] it necessary that you should renew and extend your remonstrances on the subject. In aid of the means for this purpose furnished by the information and instructions given you from time to time, I forward you an examination of it, just published, in which you will find a variety of facts and views of the British principle and proceedings, that may be made to bear against them. I will forward also in a few days copies of sundry memorials from the Merchants of our maritime Cities, explaining the wrongs done them, and the disgust with which they are filled. These with other documents accompanying them will assist your endeavours to make on the British Government the impressions which the occasion calls for.

I shall only add at present that notwithstanding the conviction of the illegality of the British principal, which becomes more and more evident the more it is investigated, the President so far yields to a spirit of conciliation as to be still willing to concur in the adjustment on the point authorized in your instructions of Jany 5th 1804; but expects and enjoins that you will be particularly careful to use such forms of expression as will furnish no pretext for considering an exception of the direct trade between a belligerent nation and its Colonies as *declaratory* of a limitation of the neutral right and not as a positive stipulation founded on considerations of expediency. I have the honor to be &c

## Document 3-b†

### Madison's Anonymous Pamphlet

IN times of peace, among all nations, their commercial intercourse is under no other restrictions than what may be imposed by their respective laws, or their mutual compacts. No one or more nations can justly controul the commerce between any two or more of the others.

When war happens between any two or more nations, a question arises, in what respect it can affect the commerce of nations not engaged in the war?

Between the nations not engaged in the war, it is evident that the commerce cannot be affected at all by a war between others.

As a nation not engaged in the war remains in the same relations of amity and of commercial pursuits with each of the belligerent nations as existed prior to the war, it would seem that the war could not affect the intercourse between the neutral and either of the belligerent nations; and that the neutral nation might treat and trade with either or both the belligerent nations, with the same freedom as if no war had arisen between them. This, as the general rule, is sufficiently established.

But inasmuch as the trade of a neutral nation with a belligerent nation

†From: *Examination of the British Doctrine, which subjects to capture a Neutral Trade Not Open in Time of Peace*, pp. 1-5, 133-38.

might, in certain special cases, affect the safety of its antagonist, usage, founded on the principle of necessity, has admitted a few exceptions to the general rule.

Thus, all instruments of war, going into the hands of one belligerent nation, may be intercepted on the high seas by its adversary.

In like manner, a neutral trade with a place actually besieged is liable to be interrupted by the besiegers.

It is maintained also on one side, though strongly contested on the other, that the property of a nation at war, in a neutral ship, may be seized and condemned by the enemy of that nation.

To these exceptions Great Britain has undertaken to add another, as important as it is new. She asserts a right to intercept the trade of neutrals with her enemies in all cases where the trade, as it respects the ship, the cargo, or even the individual port of destination, was not as free before the war as it is made during the war.

In applying this doctrine the British government and courts have not as yet extended it beyond the trade of neutrals on the coasts and with the colonies of enemies.

... But the latitude in which it is avowed, and carried into operation, sufficiently demands the serious attention of all nations; but more than any, that of the United States, whose commerce more than any is the victim to this belligerent pretension. To prepare the way for this examination, several remarks are to be premised.

First. The general rule being, that the trade between a neutral and belligerent nation is as free as if the latter were at peace with all nations, and the cases in which it is not as free being exceptions to the general rule, the exceptions, according to a received maxim of interpretation, are to be taken strictly against those claiming the benefit of the exceptions, and favourably for those claiming the benefit of the general rule.

Secondly. The exceptions being founded on a principle of necessity, in opposition to ordinary right, the necessity ought to be evident and urgent. In proportion as the necessity may be doubtful, and still more in proportion as the sacrifice of neutral interests would exceed the advantage to the belligerent, the exception fails.

Thirdly. The progress of the law of nations, under the influence of science and humanity, is mitigating the evils of war, and diminishing the motives to it, by favouring the rights of those remaining at peace, rather than of those who enter into war. Not only are the laws of war tempered between the parties at war, but much also in relation to those at peace.

.... With what astonishment, then, must the neutral world now learn, from the decision of sir William Scott on the 23d of July, 1805, that according to the rule of law just laid down, after much deliberation by the lords of appeals, "the circumstances of landing the goods, or securing the duties, do not furnish complete evidence of the termination of the voyage;" and that without this complete evidence derived from the *original intention* of the importing voyage, the voyage from the neutral port will be treated as the continuance of the voyage from the colony to the mother country.

This political change in the judicial rules of condemnation admits no other satisfactory than a commercial explanation: for the loss of character which it induces is a greater sacrifice than could be made to the cupidity of cruisers, or the value of their prizes to the public.

The whole course, indeed, of modifications pursued by the instructions, and by the decisions of the courts, as they appear from day to day, can leave no doubt that the primary object with Great Britain has been to transfer to herself as large a share as possible of the commercial advantages yielded by the colonies of her enemies. An absolute monopoly was embarrassed by the irresistible pretensions of neutral countries; more especially of the United States, whose neighborhood and habits of intercourse, together with other considerations, forbade a perseverance in the original attempt to exclude them. They were accordingly the first of the neutral nations towards which a relaxation was afforded. The relaxation, after considerable delay, was extended, by the instruction of 1798, to the neutral nations of Europe. That instruction was founded on a compromise between the interest and the prudence of Great Britain. It permitted neutral nations to trade *directly* with the colonies of her enemies, without trading in colonial productions with one another; and permitted all of them to carry those productions *directly* to *Great Britain*. This arrangement was manifestly calculated to limit the importations of each neutral country to the amount of its own consumption; and consequently to turn the immense residue of colonial wealth, through neutral vessels, into her own market; whence it might be dispensed, under her own regulations, to the neutral countries of Europe having no direct commerce with the West Indies, and even to the belligerent nations whose commerce with their respective colonies she has as completely destroyed, as she has their commerce with foreign countries. The arrangement was specious, but proved to be deceptive. It was expected, that the expense and delay of a circuitous trade through the United States would prevent importations and re-exportations interfering with the projected trade directly from the West Indies to herself; and, so long as this expectation was in any degree indulged, the right of re-exportation was admitted, though reluctantly, both by the government and the courts. Experience, however, finally showed, that the activity, the capital, and the economy, employed by the American traders overpowered the disadvantages incident to the circuit through the ports of United States, and secured to them the profits of supplying Europe with the colonial productions of her enemies. In proportion as this unforeseen operation disclosed itself, the *commercial* jealousy of Great Britain began to take alarm. Obstructions were to be thrown in the way of importations. Re-exportations were seen with growing discontent. The idea of continuity, by which two voyages were consolidated into one, came into vogue. The vice-admiralty courts, regardless of the superior decisions in England, would not allow that the landing of a cargo, and paying the duties, protected it against condemnation. At length appeared the *sentence of sir William Scott*, above cited  carrying into effect the construction of the inferior courts, as having been deliberately sanctioned by the lords of appeal. The doctrine established by that decision has been followed by other decisions and *dicta*, at first requiring the re-exportation in another ship, then a previous sale of the articles in the neutral market, then other conditions, one after another, as they were found necessary; till it is finally understood that no precautions whatever are to bar the cruisers from suspecting, nor the courts from scrutinising, the intention of the original importer, and that the proof of this intention, not to re-export the articles, is to fall on the claimant. To fill up the measure of judicial despotism, these wanton innovations are now extended to vessels returning from the belligerent mother countries, as well as to those going thither from the United States; with the addition of demands of proof, never before heard of in prize courts, on points utterly unknown to the law of nations.

These unexampled and vexatious proceedings manifestly have in view *the entire obstruction* of colonial re-exports from the United States; and it would be more candid in Great Britain, if not more just, to give public notice, at once, that in all such cases capture and condemnation would be authorised.

Her present system, as subsidiary to the extension of her commerce, will be still further seen in her concurrent measures, of a type not less extraordinary than that of any which have preceded them.

According to the instructions issued within the period of the existing war, or to the received interpretation of them, the permission given the neutrals by those of 1798, to carry the produce of enemy's colonies directly therefrom to Great Britain, has not been continued. At first view, this might appear to be inconsistent with the policy ascribed to her in obstructing re-exportations from the United States. The act of parliament, of June 27, 1805, however, which has been already noticed, changes this appearance of departure from that policy into a new proof, and even an extension of that policy. By the regulations of that act a direct trade is opened between the British colonies in the West Indies and those of her enemies; and her enemies themselves are invited to enter into the trade. Whilst neutrals, therefore, are excluded from carrying colonial produce directly from the colonies to Great Britain, the commercial views of Great Britain are answered by the substitution of another channel through her own colonies; with the additional advantage of a *monopoly to her own ships*, in the transportation from her colonies across the Atlantic; and for the sake of this advantage, or for that of repressing the growth of neutral rivalship, or on both these accounts, she has been willing to encounter all the reproach of cultivating an avowed commerce with her enemies, in the very moment of laying new restrictions on that of neutrals with them.

.... The system of Great Britain may, therefore, now be considered as announced to all the world without disguise, and by the most solemn acts of her government. Her navy having destroyed the trade of her enemies, as well between the mother countries and their colonies as between the former and neutral countries and her courts, by putting an end to re-exportations from neutral countries, reducing the importations into these to the mere amount of their own consumption—the immense surplus of productions accumulating in the American possessions of her enemies can find no outlet but through the free ports provided for it, nor any other market than the British market, and those to which she finds it for her interest to distribute it; with a view to which, she not only allows her enemies to trade with her possessions, but allows her own subjects to trade with her enemies. And thus, in defiance as well of her treason laws and of her trade laws, as of the rights of neutrality under the law of nations, we find her, in the just and emphatic language of the president, "taking to herself, by an inconsistency at which reason revolts, a commerce with her own enemy, which she denies to a neutral, on the ground of its aiding that enemy in the war*."

*President's message, December 3, 1805.

# 4

# A Republican View of America's Role in a World at War

The renewal of war by the English and French in 1803 soon had reverberations across the Atlantic as the belligerents plunged into a war that would be fought with words as a major weapon. Quickly perceiving that a neutral stance was demanded, Jefferson hoped that America could stay clear of involvement, although his enemies insisted that the president was a Francophile and that all his actions were those of a "Jacobin." Madison, as the chief officer in the foreign department, kept the president aware of the mounting problems of impressment, restricted commerce on the high seas, and the increasing cost to national pride of naval coercion. However, the two Republicans were unwavering in their belief that a stronger navy or a militant posture would only bring on a tide of woes that might engulf the young Republic. They preferred the more subtle approach provided by the Nonimportation Act of 1806, which was meant to force a recognition of American rights as a neutral trading nation.

The firing on the United States frigate *Chesapeake* shortly after it had put out to sea was a real test of Jefferson's determination to avoid war. Reports of the short skirmish (the *Chesapeake* fired only one shot, "for honor's sake," before surrendering to the British boarding party) sent the nation into a war frenzy, and Madison was at the president's elbow as first the reports arrived, then the public reacted in such anger that a war could easily have come about through a hostile message to Congress. But that was not Jefferson's way, and the manner in which the *Chesapeake* crisis first was handled tells us much about these two Republicans of what was already becoming an old school. Still enraptured in their love affair with the Republic, both the president and his secretary of state were convinced that the forbearance and moderation exhibited by the United States could furnish an example for all the world to follow. There is no doubt but that Madison discussed this reaction to the *Chesapeake* incident and was in full accord with Jefferson's view of what should be done—to seek justice by peaceable means.

## Document 4-a†

### President Jefferson to Governor William H. Cabell of Virginia

Washington, June 29, 1807

Sir

Your favor by express was safely received on Saturday night, and I am thankful to you for the attention of which it is a proof. Considering the General and State governments as co-operators in the same holy concerns, the interest and happiness of our country, the interchange of mutual aid is among the most pleasing of the exercises of our duty. Captn. Gordon 2d in command of the Chesapeake, has arrived here with the details of that affair. Yet as the precaution you took of securing us against the accident of wanting information, was entirely proper, & the expense of the express justly a national one, I have directed him to be paid here, so that he is enabled to refund any money you may have advanced him. Mr. Gallatin & Genl. Dearborne happening to be absent, I have asked their immediate attendance here, and I expect them this day. We shall then determine on the course which the exigency and our constitutional powers call for. Whether the outrage is a proper cause for war, belonging exclusively to Congress, it is our duty not to commit them by doing anything which would have to be retracted. We may, however, exercise the powers entrusted to us for preventing future insults within our harbors, & claim firmly satisfaction for the past. This will leave Congress free to decide whether war is the most efficacious mode of redress in our case, or whether, having taught so many other useful lessons to Europe, we may not add that of showing them that there are peaceable means of repressing injustice, by making it the interest of the aggressor to do what is just, and abstain from future wrong. It is probable you will hear from us·in the course of the week. I salute you with great esteem and respect.

## Document 4-b‡

### Madison to Monroe

Dept. of State
July 6 1807

Sir

The documents herewith inclosed ... explain the hostile attack with the insulting pretext for it, lately committed near the Capes of Virga. by the British ship of war the Leopard on the American frigate the Chesapeake. [One] is a copy of the Proclamation issued by the President interdicting [sic], in consequence of that outrage, the use of our waters and every other accomodation, to all British armed ships.

This enormity is not a subject for discussion. The immunity of a National ship of war from every species and purpose of search on the high seas, has

†From: Ford, ed., *Writings of Jefferson*, vol. 9, pp. 87-88.

‡From: Madison Papers, Library of Congress, Washington, D.C.

never been contested by any nation. G. B. would be second to none in resenting such a violation of her rights, & such an insult to her flag. . . .

But the present case is marked by circumstances which give it a peculiar die. The seamen taken from the Chesapeake had been ascertained to be native Citizens of the U. States; and this fact was made known to the bearer of the demand, and doubtless, communicated by him to his commander previous to the commencement of the attack. It is a fact also, affirmed by two of the men with every appearance of truth that they had been impressed from American vessels into the British frigate from which they escaped, and by the third, that having been impressed from a British Merchant ship, he had accepted the recruiting bounty under that duress, and with a view to alleviate his situation, till he could escape to his own Country. Add that the attack was made during a period of negociation, & in the midst of friendly assurances from the B. Governmt.

The printed papers herewith sent will enable you to judge of the spirit which has been roused by the occasion. It pervades the whole community, is abolishing the distinctions of party, and regarding only the indignity offered to the sovereignty & flag of the nation, and the blood of Citizens so wantonly and wickedly shed, demands in the loudest tone, an honorable reparation.

With this demand you are charged by the President. The tenor of his proclamation will be your guide in reminding the British Govt. of the uniform proofs given by the U. S. of their disposition to maintain faithfully every friendly relation. . . . till at length no alternative is left but a voluntary satisfaction on the part of G. B. or a resort to means depending on the U. S. alone.

The exclusion of all armed ships whatever from our waters is in fact so much required by the vexations and dangers to our peace experienced from their visits, that the Président makes it a special part of the charge to you, to avoid laying the U. S. under any species of restraint from adopting that remedy. Being extended to all Belligerent nations, none of them could of right complain; and with the less reason, as the policy of *all* nations has limited the admission of foreign ships of war into their ports, to such numbers as being inferior to the naval force of the Country, could be readily made to respect its authority & laws. . . .

The President has an evident right to expect from the British Govt. not only an ample reparation to the U. S. in this case, but that it will be decided without difficulty or delay. Should this expectation fail, and above all, should reparation be refused, it will be incumbent on you to take the proper measures for hastening home according to the degree of urgency, all American vessels remaining in British ports; using for the purpose the mode least likely to awaken the attention of the British Government. Where there may be no ground to distrust the prudence or the fidelity of Consuls, they will probably be found the fittest vehikles for your intimations. It will be particularly requisite to communicate to our public ships in the Mediterranean the state of appearances if it be such as ought to influence their movements.

All negociation with the British Govt on other subjects will of course be suspended untill satisfaction on this be so pledged & arranged as to render negociation honorable. . . .

# 5

# Jefferson and Madison Favor an Embargo, 1807

The Nonimportation Act of 1806 was a failure, and the *Chesapeake* affair proved that the British navy could manhandle the tiny American naval force at will. Still the threat of war in July 1807 passed. Toward the end of the year, however, the Jefferson-Madison plan for a self-inflicted embargo was revealed to Congress and passed on December 22. The American people "hoped to escape the necessity of fighting under any circumstances whatever, [and were] anxiously looking for some expedient, or compromise, which would reconcile a policy of resistance with a policy of peace. This expedient Jefferson and Madison had for fifteen years been ready to offer them" (Adams, *History*, vol. 4 p. 138). The *Leopard-Chesapeake* incident had not involved the British Order in Council of January 7, 1807, which forbade trade to any port "in the possession of France or her allies," but rather with the impressment of American seamen by the British. The British Order in Council of November 11, 1907, was a broad decree that clamped a theoretical blockade over Europe and the French colonies so that any American ship bound for a port not under British jurisdiction was fair game for the British navy. Napoleon answered with his Milan Decree of December 17, 1807 which declared that any ship which submitted to search by a British vessel or that came via England to a continental port was "denationalized" and subject to French seizure. Although the Milan Decree was not known in America when Congress acted, the earlier Berlin Decree was cited as the authority of French men-of-war to seize ships registered in the United States. Caught between the French and British millstones created by blockades both real and merely decreed, the Jefferson-Madison policy of commercial retaliation was accepted by Congress as the lesser of two evils.

*Document 5-a†*

### The Berlin Decree, November 21, 1806

Art. I.  The British islands are declared in a state of blockade.

Art. II.  All commerce and correspondence with the British islands are prohibited. In consequence, letters or packets, addressed either to England, to

†From: *State Papers and Publick Documents of the United States . . . 10 vols. (Boston, 1817), vol. 5, p. 478.*

an Englishman, or in the English language, shall not pass through the postoffice and shall be seized. . . .

Art. VII.   No vessel coming directly from England, or from the English colonies, or having been there since the publication of the present decree, shall be received into any port.

Art. VIII.   Every vessel contravening the above clause, by means of a false declaration, shall be seized, and the vessel and cargo confiscated, as if they were English property.

## Document 5-b†

### British Order in Council, November 11, 1807

Whereas certain orders, establishing an unprecedented system of warfare against this kingdom, and aimed especially at the destruction of its commerce and resources, were sometime since, issued by the government of France, by which "the British islands were declared to be in a state of blockade," thereby subjecting to capture and condemnation all vessels, with their cargoes, which should continue to trade with his majesty's dominions:

And whereas, by the same order, "all trading in English merchandise is prohibited, and every article of merchandise belonging to England, or coming from her colonies, or of her manufacture, is declared lawful prize:" . . .

His majesty is therefore pleased, by and with the advice of his privy council, to order, and it is hereby ordered, that all the ports and places of France and her allies, or of any country at war with his majesty, and all other ports or places in Europe, from which, although not at war with his majesty, the British flag is excluded, and all ports or places in the colonies belonging to his majesty's enemies, shall, from henceforth, be subject to the same restrictions in point of trade and navigation . . . as if the same were actually blockaded by his majesty's naval forces, in the most strict and rigorous manner: And it is hereby further ordered and declared, that all trade in articles which are of the produce or manufacture of the said countries or colonies, shall be deemed and considered to be unlawful; and that every vessel trading from or to the said countries or colonies, together with all goods and merchandise on board, and all articles of the produce or manufacture of the said countries or colonies, shall be captured and condemned as prize to the captors. . . .

And whereas countries not engaged in the war have acquiesced in these orders of France, prohibiting all trade in any articles the produce or manufacture of his majesty's dominions; and the merchants of those countries have given countenance and effect to those prohibitions by accepting from persons, styling themselves commercial agents of the enemy, resident at neutral ports, certain documents, termed "certificates of origin,"

†From: *Annals of Congress*, 10th Cong., 2d sess, November 11, 1807, pp. 1698-99.

being certificates obtained at the ports of shipment, declaring that the articles of the cargo are not of the produce or manufacture of his majesty's dominions, or to that effect. . . .

His majesty is therefore pleased . . . to order . . . that if any vessel, after reasonable time shall have been afforded for receiving notice of this his majesty's order, at the port or place from which such vessel shall have cleared out, shall be found carrying any such certificate or document as aforesaid, or any document referring to or authenticating the same, such vessel shall be adjudged lawful prize to the captor, together with the goods laden therein, belonging to the persons by whom, or on whose behalf, any such document was put on board. . . .

## Document 5-c†

# An Act Laying an Embargo on All Ships and Vessels in the Ports and Harbors of the United States

*Be it enacted.* . . . That an embargo be and hereby is laid on all ships and vessels in the ports and places within the limits or jurisdiction of the United States, cleared or not cleared, bound to any foreign port or place; and that no clearance be furnished to any ship or vessel bound to such foreign port or place, except vessels under the immediate direction of the President of the United States, as shall appear best adapted for carrying the same into full effect: *Provided,* That nothing herein contained shall be construed to prevent the departure of any foreign ship or vessel, wither in ballast, or with the goods, wares, and merchandise, on board of such foreign ship or vessel, when notified of this act.

Sec. 2. *And be it further enacted,* That during the continuance of this act, no registered or sea-letter vessel, having on board goods, wares, and merchandise, shall be allowed to depart from one port of the United States to another within the same, unless the master, owner, consignee, or factor of such vessel shall first give bond with one or more sureties to the collector of the district from which she is bound to depart, in a sum of double the value of the vessel and cargo; that the said goods, wares, and merchandise, shall be relanded in some port of the United States, dangers of sea excepted; which bond, and also a certificate from the collector where the same may be relanded, shall, by the collectors respectively, be transmitted to the Secretary of the Treasury. All armed vessels possessing public commissions from any foreign Power are not to be considered as liable to the embargo laid by this act.

†From: *Annals of Congress,* 10th Cong., 1st sess, December, 1807, vol. 1, pp. 1222-3.

# 6

# As President-Elect, Madison Tries to Save the Embargo, 1808

The reports from various state caucuses on a successor for Jefferson first alarmed the Republicans, then brought a distinct sigh of relief. In June Gallatin thought all was lost, and in August the third-ranking Republican pessimistically reported that if the embargo were not lifted by October 1, "we will lose the Presidential election." But, as Henry Adams noted, the forces that had sustained Jefferson were not going to abandon Madison. "From the moment his opponents divided themselves among three candidates, Madison had nothing to fear; but even without this good fortune he possessed an advantage that weighed decisively in his favor. The State legislatures had been chosen chiefly in the spring or summer, when the embargo was still comparatively popular; and in most cases, but particularly in New York, the legislature still chose presidential electors.... The choice of electors by the legislatures of Vermont and New York defeated all chance of overthrowing Madison; but apart from these accidents of management the result was already decided by the people of Pennsylvania. The wave of Federalist success and political revolution stopped short in New York, and once more the Democracy of Pennsylvania steadied and saved the Administration.... The Republican party by a supreme effort kept itself in office but no one could fail to see that if nine months of embargo had so shattered Jefferson's power, another such year would shake the Union itself" (Adams, *History*, vol. 4, pp. 284-87). In August the outcome was still in some doubt, but when Madison helped Jefferson prepare his last "State of the Union" message, he worked as one who was about to become the chief executive himself. Madison had not lost faith in the efficacy of the embargo but he was still flaying the dead horse—the broken-voyage rule of 1756 that he thought was the chief cause of friction between the United States and England.

Jefferson used most of the material Madison prepared for the opening portion of his message. His remaining days in the White House were few, and both Jefferson and Madison were reluctant to admit that the embargo had been a failure. "This candid and liberal experiment having thus failed.... it [still] has had the important effects of saving our mariners, and our vast mercantile property, as well as of affording time for prosecuting the defensive and provisional measures called for by the occasion. It has demonstrated to foreign nations the moderation and firmness which govern our councils, and to our citizens the necessity of uniting in support of the laws and the rights of their country; and has thus long frustrated those usurpations and spoliations which, if resisted, involved war; if submitted to, sacrificed a vital principle of our national independence" (*American State Papers; Foreign Relations*, vol. 1 pp. 71-72). Clearly the two men thought alike, trusted each other, and believed that what they had done had been right for the United States.

### Document 6-a†

### Madison to Jefferson   Montpelier, Aug. 17, 1808

...   I see that the B. Parlt. is about opening a trade between her Cols. & Europe S. of Cape Finisterre making a return cargo of Provisions, a condition; but principally I suspect to get the new market on the cont. for Sugar & Coffee. Should Spain under her Temporary Govt. revoke her Decrees, or our Embargo be on other grounds removed, that Market wd. be instantly supplied by the carriers of the U. S. without being even exposed to the British rule of '56, which applies only to an *Enemy* of G. B. Considering the narrow & selfish policy of the present Cabinet, it is possible that it may be tempted to continue its orders, lest a removal of our Embargo, should interfere with her in the new commercial prospect. But I suspect that she is still more swayed, by the hope of producing a revolution in the pub. Councils here, which might be followed by a coalition with her in the war. Yrs. with affecte. & high respect

### Document 6-b‡

### Madison's Memorandum for Jefferson Concerning the State of the Union Message   29-30 October, 1808

Our ministers at London and Paris were instructed to explain ... our disposition (1) to exercise the authority in such manner as would withdraw the pretext on which the aggressions were originally founded, and open the way for a renewal of that commercial intercourse which it was alleged on all sides had been reluctantly obstructed. As each of these Govts. had pledged its readiness to concur in renouncing a measure which reached its adversary thro' the incontestable rights of neutrals only, and as the measure had been assumed by each as a retaliation for an asserted acquiescence in the aggressions of the other, it was reasonably expected that the occasion would have been seized by both for evincing the sincerity of their professions, & for restoring to the commerce of the U. S. its legitimate freedom.

†From: Jefferson Papers, Library of Congress, Washington, D.C.

‡From: Jefferson Papers, Library of Congress.

This course so clearly dictated by justice has been taken by neither. By France no answer has been given; nor is there any indication that a favorable change in her Decrees is contemplated. To that Govt. instead of a pledge for suspending our Embargo as to France whilst left in operation as to Britain, it was thought most consistent with the condition annexed to the authority vested in the Executive, requiring a sufficient safety to our commerce, to hold out the obvious change resulting from such an Act of justice by one belligerent, and refusal of it by another, in the relations between the U. S. & the latter. To G. B. whose power on the Ocean is so ascendant, it was deemed not inconsistent with that condition, to state explicitly, that on her rescinding her orders in relation to the U. S. their trade would be opened with her, and remain shut to her enemy, in case of his failure to rescind his decrees also. The unexceptionable nature of this proposition, seemed to ensure its being received in the spirit, in which it was made; and this was the less to be doubted, as the British Orders in Council, had not only been referred for their vindication to an acquiescence on the part of the U. S. no longer to be pretended, but as the arrangement proposed, whilst it resisted the illegal Decrees of France, involved moreover substantially, the precise advantages professedly aimed at by the B. Orders. The arrangement has, nevertheless, been explicitly rejected, the controverted fact being assured, that the Enemy of G. B. was the original aggressor; and the extraordinary doctrine maintained, that, without regard to any just interpositions of the neutral agst. the aggressors, w[ithou]t specifically effecting a revocation of his Acts, the injured belligerent has a right to continue his retaliations against the neutral.

This candid and liberal experiment having thus failed, and no other event having occurred, on which a suspension of the Embargo by the Executive, was authorized it necessarily remains in the extent originally given to it. We have the satisfaction however to reflect, that in return for the privations imposed by the measure, and which our fellow Citizens in general have borne with patriotism, it has had the important effects of saving our vast mercantile property and our mariners; as well as of affording time for prosecuting the defensive & provisional measures required on the part of the U. S. Whilst on another hand, the course pursued by them, will have demonstrated to foreign nations the moderation & firmness which govern their Councils and have confirmed in all their Citizens the motives which ought to unite them in support of the laws & the rights of their Country. To these considerations may be added, that the Measure has thus long frustrated those usurpations & spoliations which if resisted involved war; if submitted to, sacrificed a vital principle of our national Independence.

Under a continuance of the belligerent measures which have overspread the ocean with danger, it will be with the wisdom of Congs. to decide on the course best adapted to such a state of things; and bringing with them as they do from every part of the Union the sentiments of our Constituents, my confidence is strengthened that in forming this decision, they will, with an unerring regard to the essential rights & interests of the nation, weigh & compare the painful alternatives out of which a choice is to be made. Nor should I do justice to the virtues which on other occasions, have marked the character of the American people, if I did not cherish an equal confidence, that the Alternative chosen, whatever it may be, will be maintained with all the fortitude & patriotism which the crisis ought to inspire. . . .

# 7

# A Federalist Exposé Embarrasses Madison, 1808

In the fall of 1808, Madison had turned over to the Senate certain diplomatic dispatches from William Pinkney and John Armstrong, the American ministers in London and Paris. These were considered extremely confidential documents that had been discussed in secret sessions (after a Federalist move to make them public failed), and with his high sense of honor Madison assumed that there would not be a breach of the trust. However, the *Columbian Centinel* published the letters as proof of what appeared to be Madison's duplicity. Pinkney reported some indications that the British were willing to bend on the matter of the Orders in Council, while Armstrong's letters told a tale of French avarice and high-handedness that seemed to bear out the Federalists' contentions about the two great powers. No doubt Madison was furious when the news leaked out , and he probably agreed with other Republicans that the culprit who had passed the letters to editor Benjamin Russell had been Senator Timothy Pickering, "the high priest of Federalism." Pickering denied the charges, of course, but the damage was done at about the same time that election returns showed that Madison was to be our fourth president.

### Document†

## Madison to William Pinkney

*private*

Dear Sir            Washington Decr. 9. 1808

The October Packet having arrived before the sailing of the one bound from New York, Mr. Erskine has detained the latter a few days on that account. It enables me to add the gazettes containing a report of the debates &c. in Congs. subsequent to the dates already forwarded to N. York. . . . I have already mentioned to you that your private letter of     together with one from Genl. Armstrong, were confidentially communicated to Congs. with the reasons which led to that liberty, particularly with yours. I had

---

†From: Madison to William Pinkney, December 9, 1808, letter owned by Mrs. Laurence R. Carlton, Baltimore, Maryland, 1969.

thought it impossible that the deposit could be unsafe in their hands; speaking for itself, as it did, its manifest & irresistable claims to confidence, and going, as it did, under that solemn injunction from the President. You will find nevertheless, among the proceedings of the House, an elaborate effort to convert the conditional property it had in the communications, into an absolute one, and to defy all the palpable & serious objections to a disclosure of them to the world. Fortunately the effort failed by a majority which justified the reliance which had been put on the honor and discretion of the Body. I feel inexpressible mortification however in being obliged to add, that both have been, most unexpectedly violated by an individual member, who as you will see by the inclosed paper, has taken on himself, to write the substance of both letters to correspondents, who have had the folly or the wickedness to send it to the newspaper, with both their names & the name of the writer. Whether the House will take any steps for vindicating its honor by punishing the offender, I can not say. Having failed to do it in other cases, where the breach of confidence was chargeable to the worst motives, it is the more improbable, that they will be rigorous in a case not marked by mischievous views, and where the publication appears to be the act of the receivers, not of the writer of the letter. But whatever course may be taken by Congs. I find myself unable to express my concern at what has happened, or to offer an adequate apology for the unauthorized step on my part without which it could not have happened. I can only throw myself on your goodness, and appeal to the happy impressions made within doors, both with respect to the public & myself; and which, if the publicity were confined to our own Country, would, as far as the difference between the original & Mr. Sawyer's abstract will permit, be equal[ly] happy without doors. Mr. Erskine has of course a diplomatic eye to the publication, and will transmit it of course to Mr. Canning. He is aware however that a newspaper is no authority of any sort; and an abstract, probably from memory, by any individual, no authority for the contents of the originals. And so far as any of the observations ascribed to you, may be offensive to the British Govt. it is certainly true, that they ought to be less so, than the tenor of Mr. Canning's letter of 23 Sepr. justly is to this Govt. . . .

# 8

# The Embargo Abandoned, but the Economic Coercion Policy Remains Alive, 1809

New England Federalists thundered that the Embargo Act was ruining the country, and the fall in commercial activity was paralleled by a drop in some farm prices. Jefferson was no longer in a fighting mood, as he was ready to move back to Monticello and let Madison become the champion of old-line republicanism. An odd coalition in Congress was willing to listen to the Federalists, who publicly claimed the embargo was a national disgrace and privately believed that its repeal would smash the Republicans. "Defeat the accursed measure now, and you will not only restore commerce, agriculture, and all sorts of business activity, but you save the country from a British war," Timothy Pickering pleaded. "The power of the present miserable rulers—I mean their power to do material mischief—will then be annihilated" (Adams, *History*, vol. 4, p. 408). In their final assault on the Embargo Act, the Federalists used all their powers of rhetoric to make it seem that the Republicans had been less than candid about the purposes of an embargo. Representative Josiah Quincy did his utmost to embarrass Jefferson and Madison as the Congress moved to abandon the embargo, while John Wayles Eppes (Jefferson's son-in-law and a Virginia representative) came back in rebuttal. Within a few weeks, the embargo was dead, but the Republicans managed to pass as a substitute the Nonintercourse Act of 1809, which left Madison with the discretionary power to suspend the act if either France or England revoked their edicts.

*Document 8-a†*

# Josiah Quincy's Attack on the Embargo Act, 1809

[Mr. Quincy] ... Now I do not think I state my position too strongly when I say that not a man in this House deemed the embargo intended chiefly as a measure of coercion on Great Britain; that it was to be made permanent at all hazards, until it had effected that object; and that nothing else effectual was to be done for the support of our maritime rights. If any individual was influenced by such motives, certainly they were not those of a majority of this House. Now, sir, on my conscience, I do believe that these were the motives and intentions of Administration when they recommended the embargo to the adoption of this House. Sir, I believe these continue to be still their motives and intentions. And if this were fairly understood by the people to be the fact, I do not believe that they would countenance the continuance of such an oppressive measure, for such a purpose, without better assurance than has ever yet been given to them, that, by adherence to this policy, the great and real object of it will be effected.

The proposition which I undertake to maintain consists of three particulars. First. That it was, and is, the intention of Administration to coerce Great Britain by the embargo, and that this and not precaution, is, and was, the principal object of the policy. Second. That it was, and is intended to persevere in this measure until it effect, if possible, the proposed object. Third. That it was and is the intention of Administration to do nothing else effectual in support of our maritime rights ...

... It was necessary, therefore, in the United States, to resort early to the idea of coercion, and to press it vigorously; otherwise, the people of America could not be induced to endurance beyond the time when the reason of precaution had ceased. In America, therefore, it was coercion; but in Great Britain the state of things was altogether the reverse. Administration knew perfectly well, not only from the character of the British nation, but, also, from the most common principles of human nature, that once present this embargo to it as a measure of coercion, to compel it to adopt or retract any principle of adopted policy, and there was an end to negotiation. It would have been like laying a drawn sword upon the table, and declaring, "yield us what we demand, or we will push it to the hilt in your vitals." In such case, it was perfectly apparent that there could be received, from an independent nation, but one answer: "Take away your sword; withdraw your menace; while these continue, we listen to nothing!" Aware of this inevitable consequence, Administration not only aver that it is precaution, but, even condescend to deny it is anything else, by declaring that it is this, and this only. Thus, in Great Britain, precaution was the veil under which a sword was passed into her side. But, in the United States, coercion was the palatable liquor with which Administration softened and gargled the passage, while it thrust, at the point of the bayonet, the bitter pill of embargo down the

†From: *Annals of Congress*, 10th Cong., 2d sess., pp. 1107-19.

throats of the American people. It is this variation of the avowed motive, to suit the unquestionable diversity of the state of things in this country and Great Britain, combined with the fact that the embargo is continued long after the plea of precaution has ceased to be effectual, that produces a perfect conviction in my mind that precaution was little more than the pretext, and that coercion was, in fact, the principal purpose of the policy. Indeed, how is it possible to conclude otherwise, when the very mode of argument adopted in each country was the only one that could have made coercion successful, and the very one which would have been avoided, if precaution had been the real and only motive?

Again, sir, you talk of going to war against Great Britain, with, I believe, only one frigate, and five sloops of war, in commission! And yet you have not the resolution to meet the expense of the paltry, little navy, which is rotting in the Potomac. Already we have heard it rung on this floor, that if we fit out that little navy our Treasury will be emptied. If you had ever a serious intention of going to war, would you have frittered down the resources of this nation, in the manner we witness? You go to war, with all the revenue to be derived from commerce annihilated; and possessing no other resource than loans or direct or other internal taxes? You! a party that rose into power by declaiming against direct taxes and loans? Do you hope to make the people of this country, much more foreign nations, believe that such is your intention when you have reduced your revenue to such a condition? [Mr. G. W. CAMPBELL asked the gentleman, if he could tell how much money there was now in the Treasury. Mr. QUINCY continued.] My memory has not, at present at command the precise sum, but perhaps twelve or thirteen millions of dollars charged with the expenses and appropriations for the year. But what is this? Make any material preparation for such a war, as you must wage, if you engage with either of the European Powers, and your whole Treasury is exhausted. I am not now examining the present state of our finances. But I would address myself to men of sense, and ask them to examine the adequacy of our revenues, in their future product, to the inevitable exigencies of war. Sir, you have no other resources, commerce being gone, than loans or internal taxes. Great Britain and France know this fact as well as you. Nothing can be conducted in such a country as ours, without public notoriety. The general resources of our country are as well known in Europe as they are here. But we are about to raise an army of fifty thousand volunteers. For what purpose? I have heard gentlemen say "we can invade Canada." But, sir, does not all the world, as well as you, know that Great Britain holds, as it were, a pledge for Canada? And one sufficient to induce you to refrain from such a project, when you begin seriously to weigh all the consequences of such invasion? I mean that pledge which results from the defenceless state of your seaport towns. For what purpose would you attack Canada? For territory? No. You have enough of that. Do you want citizen refugees? No. You would be willing to dispense with them. Do you want plunder? This is the only hope an invasion of Canada can offer you. And is it not very doubtful whether she could not, in one month, destroy more property on your seaboard, than you can acquire by the most successful invasion of that Province? Sir, in this state of things, I cannot hear such perpetual outcries about war, without declaring my opinion concerning them. . . . [Quincy concluded by urging an immediate repeal of the Embargo Act. Then Jefferson's son-in-law, John Wayles Eppes, spoke in rebuttal.]

Mr. EPPES said that he had no hope, at this late hour of the day, after the House had been so long amused with an eloquent oration, abounding with tropes, figures, and well turned periods, that he could offer anything calculated to interest or amuse them. I cannot, however, said he, suppress the sentiment I feel as hearing a gentleman, in the present situation of his country, attempt to place in a degraded point of view the resources of the nation, and level exclusively at the Administration of his own Government, that asperity which ought to be confined to the belligerent nations. To a man who knew nothing of the foreign relations of this country, it would appear, from the speech of the gentleman from Massachusetts, that peace, prosperity, and every other blessing, would attend the removal of the embargo. No person, from his speech, could suppose that the sovereignty and independence of this nation was in danger from the atrocious and unprincipled conduct of foreign nations. The embargo is the cause of all our difficulties! Nothing but a removal of the embargo is necessary to re-establish the unrivalled prosperity of the nation! . . . What has the gentleman told you? You cannot carry the nation into war; you have neither resources nor men; will this country resort to direct taxes or loans? Will the party that came into power by opposing direct taxes and loans, resort to them? They cannot; whenever they do they must go out. It was neither direct taxes or loans which lost to the Federal party the confidence of the people. The prodigal expenditure of public money, which produced the necessity of taxes and loans, deprived them of the public confidence. The Republican party came in as the friends of a proper and a niggardly system of economy; on the ground of attachment to the rights of the nation individually and collectively; neither the people or the party will shrink from that species of expense which is necessary to maintain the independence and rights of the nation. That species of niggardly economy, which could put money in competition with the independence of the nation, I for one disclaim. It would be disclaimed by the whole of the Republican party. By a judicious management of our funds we have acquired credit, that is equal to our wants; we can command without difficulty and without taxes, whatever sum may be necessary to assert and maintain our rights; when the period of difficulty shall have passed, it can be discharged honestly, as our debts heretofore contracted have been, without new taxes or burdens on the people. We possess a credit superior to that of any other nation, and we deserve it. The gentleman, in speaking of his political opponents, has said, by their deeds shall you know them. Apply this principle to the ground taken by the gentleman. Will you, says he, with 170 gunboats fight Great Britain? Will you march into Canada and take possession of her territories? They have it in their power to punish your rashness? they will destroy your seaport towns. This is the language of an American Representative, when this nation is assailed by foreign danger; make war, and punishment awaits you; you have no army; no effective militia; no resources; you mean not to assert the rights of the nation; your object is political deception.

The gentleman from Massachusetts has brought into this discussion what he calls the reasons for laying the embargo, and has attempted to show that the real grounds of the measure have not been avowed by the Administration. He draws this conclusion from the arguments used on this floor in support of the measure. 1. That it would preserve our commercial capital, 2. That it would prevent immediate war. 3. That it would coerce Great Britain. 4. That it would have a good effect on Mr. Rose's negotiation. 5. That Bonaparte was asserting the maritime rights of the world, and that it would go in aid of that assertion. That the embargo did preserve from ruin our commercial capital, and that it did prevent war, are facts admitted by all unprejudiced men; that it produced great sensibility and alarm on the part of the British Ministry, we know. The inducement held out to our citizens to violate the laws of their country proves it. When did the British Ministry lose this sensibility? When it was discovered that, by means of their agents and subjects here, the law could be evaded. As to the operation of the embargo on the negotiation of Mr. Rose, this is entirely new to me. It is the first time I have ever heard this assigned as one of the grounds on which it was supported. As to the mission of Mr. Rose, it was a mere political juggle on the part of the British Ministry. It was intended to palsy the feeling of the nation as to the outrage on the Chesapeake; it produced that effect. The fifth ground, as to Bonaparte, I understand the gentleman from Massachusetts to have withdrawn. If the gentleman has withdrawn it, I will forbear to remark on it. . . .

*Document 8-b†*

## Representative Wilson Cary Nicholas to Madison

Febry. 6th [1809]

My dear Sir

At the beginning of the Session we cou'd have carried any plan connected with the repeal of the Embargo in the course of it. It has been our misfortune that the various expedients have been offered too late. The only honorable course was from Embargo to war—I fear we cannot now obtain it, and I fear we must submit to the plan least disgraceful, in which we can unite the greatest number of votes. All that is left for us is to chuse between a repeal of the Embargo to take effect at or before the day that congress is to meet in May; the repeal on the 4th. of March with or without arming Merchant

---

†From:  Madison Papers, Library of Congress.

Vessels, with a power to the president to grant letters of Marque & reprisal if any of our vessels are attacked &c. There wou'd be a very strong vote to issue letters of Marque and reprisal when the embargo shall cease, but I fear we cou'd not carry it. If we did, we show'd not have a majority of more than one or two. Or, the expedient you proposed yesterday of repealing the embargo on the 4th. of March, & passing the non intercourse law.

*Document 8-c†*

## The Nonintercourse Act of 1809

An Act to interdict the commercial intercourse between the United States and Great Britain and France, and their dependencies; and for other purposes.

Be it enacted, That from and after the passing of this act, the entrance of the harbors and waters of the United States and of the territories thereof, be, and the same is hereby interdicted to all public ships and vessels belonging to Great Britain or France. . . .

Sec. 2. That it shall not be lawful for any citizen or citizens of the United States or the territories thereof, nor for any person or persons residing or being in the same, to have any intercourse with, or to afford any aid or supplies to any public ship or vessel asaforesaid, which shall, contrary to the provisions of this act, have entered any harbor or waters within the jurisdiction of the United States or the territories thereof . . . [and] every person so offending, shall forfeit and pay a sum not less than one hundred dollars, nor exceeding ten thousand dollars; and shall also be imprisoned for a term not less than one month, nor more than one year.

Sec. 3. That from and after the twentieth day of May next, the entrance of the harbors and waters of the United States and the territories thereof be, and the same is hereby interdicted to all ships or vessels sailing under the flag of Great Britain or France, or owned in whole or in part by any citizen or subject of either. . . . And if any ship or vessel sailing under the flag of Great Britain or France . . . [should] arrive either with or without cargo, within the limits of the United States or the territories thereof, such ship or vessel, together with the cargo, if any, which may be found on board, shall be forfeited, and may be seized and condemned in any court of the United States or the territories thereof . . . .

Sec. 4; That from and after the twentieth day of May next, it shall not be lawful to import into the United States or the territories thereof, any goods, wares or merchandise whatever, from any port or place situated in Great Britain or Ireland, or in any of the colonies or dependencies of Great Britain, nor from any port or place situated in France, or in any of her colonies or dependencies, nor from any port or place in the actual possession of either Great Britain or France. Nor shall it be lawful to import into the United States, or the territories thereof, from any foreign port or place whatever, any

†From: U.S., *Statutes at Large*, vol. 2, pp. 528-31.

goods, wares or merchandise whatever, being of the growth, produce or manufacture of France, or of any of her colonies or dependencies, or being of the growth, produce or manufacture of Great Britain or Ireland, or of any of the colonies or dependencies of Great Britain, or being of the growth, produce or manufacture of any place or country in the actual possession of either France or Great Britain. . . .

Sec. 11. That the President of the United States be, and he hereby is authorized, in case either France or Great Britain shall so revoke or modify her edicts, as that they shall cease to violate the neutral commerce of the United States, to declare the same by proclamation; after which the trade of the United States, suspended by this act, and by the [embargo] . . . may be renewed with the nation so doing. . . .

Sec. 12. [So much of the embargo and supplementary acts] as forbids the departure of vessels owned by citizens of the United States, and the exportation of domestic and foreign merchandise to any foreign port or place, be and the same is hereby repealed, after March 15, 1809, except so far as they relate to Great Britain or France, or their colonies or dependencies, or places in the actual possession of either. . . .

Sec. 19. That this act shall continue and be in force until the end of the next session of Congress, and no longer; and that the act laying an embargo on all ships and vessels in the ports and harbors of the United States, and the several acts supplementary thereto, shall be, and the same are hereby repealed from and after the end of the next session of Congress.

# 9

## Madison Negotiates a Settlement with the British Minister, 1809

David Erskine came to Washington bearing the seals of office of George III's minister to his former colonies. Erskine came to succeed, and for a brief moment it appeared that he had carried out the almost impossible. With a speed that in diplomacy is almost breathtaking, Erskine thought he had settled the *Chesapeake* affair, and made arrangements for a rescinding of all the commercial restrictions on Anglo-American trade. We can only imagine the great sense of personal disappointment that Madison felt when the truth from England finally reached Washington during the summer—Canning had repudiated the Erskine negotiations, and instead of an easing of tension the clamp applied by the British navy to neutral commerce was to be tightened.

### Document 9-a†

### Madison Proclaims a Renewal of Anglo-American Trade

*By the President of the United States of America.*

*A PROCLAMATION.*

Whereas it is provided by the eleventh section of the act of Congress, entitled "An act to interdict the commercial intercourse between the United States and Great Britain and France, and their dependencies, and for other purposes;" that "in case either France or Great Britain shall so revoke or modify her edicts as that they shall cease to violate the neutral commerce of the United States," the President is authorized to declare the same by proclamation; after which the trade suspended by the said act, and by an act laying an embargo on all ships and vessels in the ports and harbors of the United States, and the several acts supplementary thereto, may be renewed with the nation so doing; and whereas the honorable David Montague Erskine, His Britannic Majesty's envoy extraordinary and minister plenipoteniary, has, by the order and in the name of his Sovereign, declared to this Government that the British orders in council of January and November, 1807, will have been withdrawn, as respects the United States, on the 10th day of June next: Now,

---

†From: *American State Papers: Foreign Relations*, vol. 3, p. 297.

therefore, I, James Madison, President of the United States, do hereby proclaim that the orders in council aforesaid will have been withdrawn on the said 10th day of June next; after which day the trade of the United States with Great Britain, as suspended by the act of Congress above mentioned, and an act laying an embargo on all ships and vessels in the ports and harbors of the United States, and the several acts supplementary thereto, may be renewed.

Given under my hand, and the seal of the United States, at Washington, [L. S.] the nineteenth day of April, in the year of our Lord one thousand eight hundred and nine, and of the independence of the United States the thirty-third.

JAMES MADISON.

By the President:

R. SMITH, *Secretary of State.*

## Document 9-b†

### Madison to John G. Jackson[1]

Washington Apl. 21. 1809

Dear Sir

The inclosed paper contains the result of what has passed between Mr. Smith & Mr. Erskine. You will see that it puts an end to the two immediate difficulties with G.B. and has the air of a policy in her, to come to a thorough adjustment. It remains to be seen whether the pride or the prudence of France is to prescribe the course which she will take in consequence of this new state of things. We have nothing from abroad, nor at home, more than is afloat in the Gazettes. Yr. respectfully &

## Document 9-c‡

### Madison to Jefferson

Washington May 30. 1809

Dear Sir

Your favor of the 22d. did not come to hand till the day before yesterday. . . . The newfangled policy of the federal party, you will have noticed, has made a considerable figure in the newspapers. Some of the Editors are resuming the Old cant, and the others will doubtless soon follow the example. Nothing could exceed the folly of supposing that the principles & opinions manifested in our foreign discussion, were not, in the main at least, common to us; unless it be the folly of supposing that such shallow hyprocrisy could deceive any one. The truth is, the sudden & unlooked for

---

†From: Jackson Collection, Indiana University Libraries, Bloomington, Ind.

[1] A Virginia congressman and kinsman of Madison's.

‡From: Madison Papers, Library of Congress.

turn of the [British] Cabinet, has thrown the party entirely off the Center. They have at present no settled plan. There is reason to believe that the leaders are soured towards England, and much less disposed than heretofore to render our interests subservient to hers. Expressions have been used by one at least of the Essex Cabinet, whether sincerely or insidiously may not be absolutely certain, from which it is inferred that a disposition exists in that quarter not even to continue the non-intercourse Act agst. France. Certain it is, that the desire of war with her is no longer manifested; that the deficiency of the English markets excites a keen appetite for a trade with the continent; and that a real uneasiness is felt lest the negociations with G. B. should end in sacrifices on our part, which they have been reproaching the Administration for not being ready to make. As one proof of their present feelings, the federal leaders shew a marked alienation from Erskine. The Elections in Massts. as well as in N.H. & N.Y. have issued unfavorably. But the smallness of the majority, and the overstrained exertions it has required, seem to depress rather than flatter the successful party. No confidence is felt in the permanency of the triumph.

Not a line has been recd. of late from any of our foreign Agents. All that is known is therefore to be gathered from the ordinary and fallacious channels. Accept my sincere respects & attachment

*Document 9-d†*

### Madison to Jefferson

Washington June 12 1809

Dr. Sir

The Pacific has just returned from G. B. bringing the accts to be seen in the Newspapers. The communications from Pinkney add little to them. The new orders, considering the time, and that the act was known on the passage of which the instructions lately executed by Erskine, was predicated, present a curious feature in the conduct of the B Cabinet. It is explained by some at the expence of its sincerity. It is more probably ascribed, I think to an awkwardness in getting out of an awkward situation, and to the policy to witholding as long as possible from France, the motive of its example, to advances on her part towards adjustment with us. The crooked proceeding seems to be operating as a check to the extravagance of credit given to G. B. for her late arrangement with us; and so far may be salutary. Be assured of my constant affection

†From: Madison Papers, Library of Congress.

*Document 9-e†*

## Madison to Jefferson
### Montpellier July 23. 1809

Dear Sir

On my arrival at O. C. House[1] on thursday I found your favor of the 12th. inst: with the document expected, & the letters from Short & Warden enclosed. . . . Mr. Shorts idea of leaving commerce to shift for itself, is not as new as he seems to think; and is liable to greater objections; in the case stated at least. A decisive objection wd. have been that the expedient would have given all the trade wanted to the power commanding the sea, whilst this would have cut off the commerce with its enemy; & thus have found an adequate motive to keep in force its obnoxious orders, as answering all its purposes. It was to be considered also as a further objection, that such an expedient would have involved our ignorant & credulous mariners, in the penalties incurred by the mercantile adventurers, without the indemnifying advantages which the latter would secure to themselves. It may be added that so formal an abandonment of the national rights, would not have borne an honorable appearance; tho' the credit would have been mitigated by examples of powerful nations, & still more by the peculiarities of the actual state of the world.

I have not recd a line from any quarter, nor even a newspaper since I left Washington. I can say nothing therefore on the score of news. . . .

It is a part of our plan to pay our respects to Monticello; but we can say nothing as yet of the time. It will afford us much gratification to welcome you here, & with all of your family, that can accompany you. Be assured of my most affectionate respects

*Document 9-f‡*

## Robert Smith to Madison
### Washn. July 24. 1809

Sir

The enclosed papers shew the temper of the B. Govt. with respect to our late arrangement with Mr. Erskine and induce a strong presumption that no adjustment consistent with our interest or our honor can be made with that infatuated nation. It would seem that Erskine is to be superseded by Mr. Jackson, who may every day be expected. You will be pleased to state to me what answer . . . I am to give to his note requesting the honor of being presented to you. . . .

---

†From: Madison Papers, Library of Congress.

[1] Orange Court House, Madison's mailing address a few miles north of Montpelier.

‡From: Madison Papers, Library of Congress.

*Document 9-g†*

## Madison to Gallatin

Montpellier July 28. 1809

Dear Sir

I have recd. yours of the 24th. The conduct of the B. Govt. in protesting the arrangement of its Minister surprizes one in spite of all their examples of folly. If it be not their plan, now that they have filled their magazines with our supplies, and ascertained our want of firmness in witholding them, to adopt openly a system of monoply & piracy, it may be hoped that they will not persist in the scandalous course in which they have set out. Supposing Erskine to have misunderstood or overstrained his instructions, can the difference between our trading directly & indirectly with Holland, account for the violent remedy applied to. the case? Is it not more probable that they have yielded to the clamors of the London Smugglers in Sugar and Coffee, whose numbers & impudence are displayed in the scandalous & successful demand from their Govt. that it should strangle the lawful trade of a friendly nation lest it should interfere with their avowed purpose of carrying on a smuggling trade with their Enemies. Such an outrage on all decency, was never before heard of, even on the shores of Africa. I have a private letter of late date from London, which says it was whispered that the Ministry were inclined to swallow the pill sent them; but that the King considered himself as insulted in what related to Berkley and positively refused his consent. This is not impossible, and may assist in explaining the phenomenon. Still, I can not but hope, in the supposition that there be no predetermined hostility agst. our commerce & navigation, that things may take another turn, under the influence of the obvious & striking considerations which advise it. The sudden disavowal of Erskine by the Ministry took place in a moment of alarm [from] the situation in which it placed them; and the confusion is strongly marked on the expedient resorted to. Whilst they acknowledge the obligation to save the Amn. Merchts. from the snare, they not only leave it open for those not going directly from the U. S. but take no notice of the Mediterranean ports opened by the arrangement & shut by their decree. This is another presumption that the Holland market alone was in their thoughts, & that on acct. of the Smugglers who awed them.

In answer to a letter to Mr. Smith, I have made a few observations on the several points for consideration; declining a return to Washington, as not necessary, but awaiting the result of your consultations on that as on other subjects. I venture to hope that my return will not be found necessary; the less so as you will be able to bring with you so full a view of the state of things, and the sentiments of your colleagues, that my decision as far as necessary, may be made as well here as at Washington. The point of most injury seems to be the effect of the failure of the arrangement on our commercial relations with G. B. If the non-intercourse with her results, and it

†From: Gallatin Papers, New York Historical Society, New York, New York.

be necessary in any mode to take official notice of it, I have thought the best to be that of a circular to the collectors, which wd. of course become public. Among the objections to a Proclamation, revoking that of April, is the quere whether that was not an act terminating the power over the subject of it. . . .

# 10

# Protests, Legislation, and Diplomacy, 1809-1810

The shock of Canning's repudiation of Erskine took some time to wear off. Meanwhile there was mounting evidence that American commerce was being plundered not only by the British and French, but also by privateers and cruisers operating under supposedly friendly flags. Not only did Madison have to eat crow and recall his proclamation of April 19, 1809, but he also had to be civil to "Copenhagen" Jackson, Erskine's replacement. The Republican dilemma Madison had inherited from Jefferson must have caused him the utmost anxiety, for the embargo had failed, the Erskine talks had led to humiliation and embarrassment, and after six years of patient effort it seemed that the United States was still treated as a second-class power with no rights on the high seas that were not conferred by the protruding cannon barrels on men-of-war. And yet, Madison was not ready to give up his republicanism and swing to the other direction by leading the Congress toward a heavy armaments program. He would wait for better times and more reasonable men in the councils of Britain and France. After long debate, Congress passed an odd piece of legislation known as Macon's Bill, No. 2, which held a carrot out on a long stick—it offered to cancel all restrictions on a belligerent power if that country would "so revoke or modify her edicts as that they shall cease to violate the neutral commerce of the United States." Napoleon had just promulgated his Rambouillet Decree in retaliation to Americar legislation and ordered the seizure of all United States vessels in French ports. Now, with Macon's Bill No. 2, both the major powers were invited to drive a further wedge between their enemy and the United States.

The reaction to Macon's Bill No. 2 was understandably mixed. The English thought the act was a confession of failure by the administration, but Federalists were pleased to send out their ships again, and southern commodities flooded the British market in a few months. Since Britain controlled the seas, the French were not able to send their merchantmen to America anyway, so a remark on the floors of Congress that the new law "held up the honor and character of this nation to the highest bidder" was to some degree true (Perkins, *Prologue to War*, p. 241). However, in war and politics a sudden change of fortunes can throw every well-laid plan into a jumble. Neither the British nor the Americans had counted on the cynicism of Napoleon Bonaparte.

*Document 10-a†*

## Protest of Philadelphia Merchants Against
## Danish Depredations, 1809

Philadelphia, October 19, 1809.

*To JAMES MADISON, President of the United States; the memorial of the subscribers, merchants and underwriters of the city of Philadelphia, respectfully represents:*

That, during the present year, and since the expiration of the embargo laws, your memorialists have fitted out and loaded or insured several vessels with valuable cargoes, destined for the ports or countries in amity with the United States, and not known to be under blockade or any restriction that would render the admission of American vessels hazardous; that some of those vessels having departed from the United States previous to the proclamation which took off the restriction from the ports of the United Kingdoms and their dependenc[i]es, took clearances *for a permitted port in Europe*, but were actually destined for a port in Russia, or some one in Denmark or Sweden.

That, notwithstanding their being furnished with all the documents and evidences of the neutral character of both vessels and cargoes, in every instance in which they have been met with by Danish cruisers they have been captured and sent into the ports, under the dominion of that nation, and, with their cargoes, have been condemned, (with very few exceptions;) and even when acquitted, the sentences have been appealed from, so as to prevent a restitution of the property, and at the last advices the whole was detained to abide the sentence of the superior tribunals. That, from the destruction or dilapidations of the papers by the captors, as well as from other circumstances, your memorialists have too much reason to apprehend an unfavorable issue of the cases; and that if the property should be distributed, no subsequent determination would enable them to recover its value, the captors being (as they understand) generally without property or responsibility.

That, besides the vessels and cargoes enumerated and specified in the schedule transmitted by your memorialists to the Department of State, there is certain information that a great number of vessels belonging to other ports of the United States have been captured, and are under like circumstances with those of your memorialists, and likely to share the same fate.

Under these circumstances, and considering the magnitude of the object, your memorialists presume to hope for the interference of Government in their behalf, by despatching a public vessel, and a person to present the case to the Danish Government, or such other measures as the wisdom of the

†From: *American State Papers: Foreign Relations*, vol. 3, pp. 332-33.

President may deem proper, which with the proofs ready to be adduced by your memorialists, warrant the expectation that the property would be restored.

### Document 10-b†

## Madison Asks for the Recall of Erskine's Replacement; William Pinkney to Lord Wellesley, 1810

My Lord:                                    Great Cumberland Place, *January* 2, 1810.

In the course of the official correspondence which has lately taken place between the Secretary of State of the United States, and Mr. Jackson, His Majesty's envoy extraordinary and minister plenipotentiary at Washington, it has unfortunately happened that Mr. Jackson has made it necessary that I should receive the commands of the President to request his recall, and that, in the mean time, the intercourse between that minister and the American Government should be suspended.

I am quite sure, my lord, that I shall best consult your lordship's wishes, and the respect which I owe to His Majesty's Government, by executing my duty on this occasion with perfect simplicity and frankness. My instructions, too, point to that course as required by the honor of the two Governments, and as suited to the confidence which they relate. With such inducements to exclude from this communication every thing which is not intimately connected with its purpose, and, on the other hand, to set forth, with candor and explicitness, the facts and considerations which really belong to the case, I should be unpardonable if I fatigued your lordship with unnecessary details, or affected any reserve.

It is known to your lordship that Mr. Jackson arrived in America, as the successor of Mr. Erskine, while disappointment, produced by the disavowal of the arrangement of the 19th of April, was yet recent, and while some other causes of dissatisfaction, which had been made to associate themselves with that disappointment, were in operation; but your lordship also knows that his reception by the American Government was marked by all that kindness and respect which were due to the representative of a sovereign, with whom the United States were sincerely desirous of maintaining the most friendly relations. . . .

Accordingly on the 9th of October, Mr. Smith addressed a letter to Mr. Jackson, in which, after stating the course of proceeding which the American Government had supposed itself entitled to expect from him with regard to the rejected arrangement and the matters embraced by it, and after recapitulating what Mr. Smith believed to have passed in their recent interviews relative to those subjects, he intimated that it was thought expedient that their further discussions, on that particular occasion, should be in writing.

†From: *American State Papers: Foreign Relations*, 3, pp. 352-55.

It is evident, my lord, from Mr. Jackson's reply of the 11th of the same month, that he received this intimation (which, carefully restricted as it was, he seems to have been willing to understand in a general sense) with considerable sensibility. He speaks of it in that reply as being without example in the annals of diplomacy; as a step against which it was fit to enter his protest; as a violation, in his person, of the most essential rights of a public minister; as a new difficulty thrown in the way of a restoration of a thorough good understanding between the two countries. . . .

[Jackson had further complicated matters by intimating that the representatives of the United States had known that Mr. Erskine was violating his instructions and despite this knowledge had proceeded to issue a proclamation that was, in effect, an act of bad faith.]

This harsh accusation, enhanced by the tone of the letter in which it appeared, was in all respects as extraordinary as it was offensive. It took the shape of an inference from facts and asseverations, which neccessarily led to the opposite conclusion. It was preferred as an answer to a claim of explanation, which Mr. Jackson professed not to be authorized by his Government to offer at all, but which he chose so to offer from himself as to convert explanation into insult. It was advanced, not only without proof, and against proof, but against all color of probability. It could scarcely have been advanced, under any conviction, that it was necessary to the case which Mr. Jackson was to maintain; for His Majesty's Government had disavowed Mr. Erskine's arrangement, according to Mr. Jackson's own representations, without any reference to the knowledge which this accusation imputed to the Government of the United States; and it need not be stated, that no allusion whatsoever was made to it by Mr. Secretary Canning, in those informal communications to me which Mr. Jackson has mentioned. It was not, moreover, to have been expected that, in the apparent state of Mr. Jackson's powers, and in the actual posture of his negotiation, he would seek to irritate where he could not arrange, and sharpen disappointment by studied and unprovoked indignity.

The course which the Government of the United States adopted on this painful occasion was such as at once demonstrated a sincere respect for the public character with which Mr. Jackson was invested, and a due sense of its own dignity. Mr. Jackson's conduct had left a feeble hope that further intercourse with him, unproductive of good as it must be, might still be reconcilable with the honor of the American Government. A fair opportunity was accordingly presented to him of making it so, by Mr. Smith's letter of the 1st of November, of which I beg leave to insert the concluding paragraph:

"I abstain, sir, from making any particular animadversions on several irrelevant and improper allusions in your letter, not at all comporting with the professed disposition to adjust in an amicable manner the differences unhappily subsisting between the two countries. But it would be improper to conclude the few observations to which I purposely limit myself, without adverting to your repetition of a language implying a knowledge, on the part of this Government, that the instructions of your predecessor did not authorize the arrangement formed by him. After the explicit and peremptory asseveration that this Government had no such knowledge, and that, with such knowledge, no such arrangement would have been entered into, the view which you have again presented of the subject makes it my duty to apprize you that such insinuations are inadmissible in the intercourse of a foreign minister with a Government that understands what it owes to itself."[1]

Whatever was the sense in which Mr. Jackson had used the expressions to which the American Government took exception, he was now aware of the sense in which they were understood; and, consequently, was called upon, if he had been misapprehended, to say so. His expressions conveyed an injurious meaning, supported, moreover, by the context, and the notice taken of them had not exceeded the bounds of just admonition. To have explained away even an imaginary affront would have been no degradation; but, when an occasion was thus offered, to qualify real and severe imputations upon the Government is called in question, to vindicate his honor and dignity, in the duty to take immediate advantage of it.

Such, however, was not Mr. Jackson's opinion. He preferred answering the appeal, which had been made to him, by reiterating with aggravations the offensive insinuation. He says, in the last paragraph of his letter of the 4th of November, to Mr. Smith, "You will find that, in my correspondence with you, I have carefully avoided drawing conclusions *that did not necessarily follow from the premises advanced by me*; and least of all should I think of uttering an insinuation where I was unable *to substantiate a fact*. To facts, such as I have become acquainted with them, I have scrupulously adhered. *In so doing, I must continue*, whenever the good faith of His Majesty's Government is called in question, to vindicate his honor and dignity, in the manner that appears to me best calculated for that purpose."

To this, my lord, there could be but one reply. Official intercourse with Mr. Jackson could no longer be productive of any effects that were not rather to be avoided than desired; and it was plainly impossible that it should continue. He was, therefore, informed by Mr. Smith, in a letter of the 8th of November, which recapitulated the inducements to this unavoidable step, that no further communications would be received from him; that the necessity of this determination would, without delay, be made known to his Government; and that, in the mean time, a ready attention would be given to any communications, affecting the interests of the two nations, through any other channel that might be substituted.

The President has been pleased to direct that I should make known this necessity to His Majesty's Government, and, at the same time, request that Mr. Jackson be recalled. . . .[1]

---

[1]It is almost certain that this letter, although signed by Smith, was actually written by Madison.

*Document 10-c†*

## Macon's Bill No. 2, 1810

[May 1, 1810]

*An Act concerning the commercial intercourse between the United States and Great Britain and France and their dependencies, and for other purposes.*

*Be it enacted.* That from and after the passage of this act, no British or French armed vessel shall be permitted to enter the harbor or waters under the jurisdiction of the United States ... except when they shall be forced in by distress. ...

Sec. 4. That in case either Great Britain or France shall, before the third day of March next, so revoke or modify her edicts as that they shall cease to violate the neutral commerce of the United States, which fact the President of the United States shall declare by proclamation, and if the other nation shall not within three months thereafter so revoke or modify her edicts in like manner, then [sections three through ten and section eighteen] ... of the act, entitled "An act to interdict the commercial intercourse between the United States and Great Britain and France. ... " shall, from and after the expiration of three months from the date of the proclamation aforesaid, be revived and have full force and effect, so far as relates to the dominions, colonies, and dependencies of the nation thus refusing or neglecting to revoke or modify her edicts in the manner aforesaid. And the restrictions imposed by this act shall, from the date of such proclamation, cease and be discontinued in relation to the nation revoking or modifying her decrees in the manner aforesaid.

*Document 10-d‡*

## Madison to William Pinkney

Washington May 23d 1810

Dear Sir

You will learn from the Department of State, as you must have anticipated, our surprise that the answer of Lord Wellesley, to your very just and able view of the case of Jackson, corresponded so little with the impressions of that Minister manifested in your first interviews with him. ... The elections which have since taken place in the Eastern States, and which have been materially influenced by the affair of Jackson and the spirit of party connected with it, are the strongest of proofs, that the measure of the Executive [in seeking Jackson's recall] coincided with the feelings of the Nation.

... The Act of Congress [Macon's Bill No. 2] transmitted from the Department of State, will inform you of the footing on which our relations to the Belligerent powers were finally placed. The experiment now to be made,

†From: United States, *Statutes at Large*, vol. 2, pp. 605-606.
‡From: Madison Papers, Library of Congress.

of a commerce with both, unrestricted by our laws, has resulted from causes which you will collect from the debates, and from your own reflections. The new form of appeal to the policy of Great Britain and France on the subject of the Decrees and Orders, will most engage your attention. However feeble it may appear, it is possible that one or other of those powers may allow it more effect than was produced by the overtures heretofore tried. As far as pride may have influenced the reception of these, it will be the less in the way, as the law in its present form may be regarded by each of the parties, if it so pleases, not as a coercion or a threat to itself, but as a promise of attack on the other. G. Britain indeed may conceive that she has now a compleat interest in perpetuating the actual state of things, which gives her the full enjoyment of our trade and enables her to cut it off with every other part of the World; at the same time that it increases the chance of such resentments in France at the inequality, as may lead to hostilities with the United States. But on the other hand, this very inequality, which France would confirm by a state of hostilities with the U. States, may become a motive with her to turn the tables on G. Britain by compelling her either to revoke her orders, or to lose the commerce of this Country. An apprehension that France may take this politic course would be a rational motive with the B. Govt. to get the start of her. Nor is this the only apprehension that merits attention. Among the inducements to the experiment of an unrestricted commerce now made, were two which contributed essentially to the majority of votes in its favor; first a general hope, favored by daily accounts from England, that an adjustment of differences there, and thence in France, would render the measure safe & proper; second, a willingness in not a few, to teach the advocates for an open trade, under actual circumstances, the folly, as well as degradation of their policy. At the next meeting of Congress, it will be found, according to present appearances, that instead of an adjustment with either of the Belligerents, there is an increased obstinacy in both; and that the inconveniences of the Embargo, and non-intercourse, have been exchanged for the greater sacrifices as well as disgrace, resulting from a submission to the predatory systems in force. It will not be wonderful therefore, if the passive spirit which marked the late session of Congress, should at the next meeting be roused to the opposite point; more especially as the tone of the Nation has never been as low as that of its Representatives, and as it is rising already under the losses sustained by our Commerce in the Continental ports, and by the fall of prices in our produce at home, under a limitation of the market, to Great Britain. Cotton I perceive is down at 10 or 11 cents in Georgia. The great mass of Tobacco is in a similar situation. And the effect must soon be general, with the exception of a few articles which do not at present, glut the British demand. Whether considerations like these will make any favorable impression on the British Cabinet, you will be the first to know. Whatever confidence I may have in the justness of them, I must forget all that has past before I can indulge very favorable expectations. Every new occasion seems to countenance the belief, that there lurks in the British Cabinet, a hostile feeling towards this Country, which will never be eradicated during the present Reign; nor overruled, whilst it exists, but by some dreadful pressure from external or internal causes.

With respect to the French Govt. we are taught by experience to be equally distrustful. It will have however the same opportunity presented to it, with the British Govt., of comparing the actual state of things, with that which would be produced by a repeal of its Decrees; and it is not easy to find any plausible motive to continue the former as preferable to the latter. A worse state of things, than the actual one, could not exist for France, unless her preference be for a state of War. If she be sincere either in her propositions relative to a chronological revocation of illegal Edicts against Neutrals, or to a pledge from the United States not to submit to those of Great Britain, she aught [sic] at once to embrace the arrangement held out by Congress; the renewal of a non-intercourse with Great Britain being the very species of resistance most analogous to her professed views. . . .

## Document 10-e†

### Madison to Jefferson

Washington May 25. 1810

Dear Sir

. . . A former Natl. Intellr. will have given you our last communications from G. B. That of this morning exhibits our prospects on the side of F. The late confiscations by Bonaparte, comprize robbery, theft, & breach of trust, and exceed in turpitude any of his enormities, not wasting human blood. This scene on the continent, and the effect of English monopoly, on the value of our produce, are breaking the charm attached to what is called fair trade, foolishly by some, & wickedly by others. We are looking hourly, for the "John Adams." There is a *possibility*, that the negociations on foot at Paris, may vary our prospects there. The change, wd. be better perhaps, if the last act of Cong. were in the hands of Armstrong; which puts our trade on the worst possible footing for France: but at the same time, puts it in the option of her, to revive the non-intercourse agst. England. There is a *possibility* also that the views of the latter may be somewhat affected by the recent elections; it being pretty certain that the change in the tone of Wellesly from that first manifested to Pinkney, was in part at least, produced by the intermediate intelligence from the U. S. which flattered a fallicious reliance on the British party here. . . .

†From: Madison Papers, Library of Congress.

*Document 10-f†*

## Madison to Jefferson

Washington June 22. 1810

Dear Sir

... On the first publication of the dispatches by the J. Adams, so strong a feeling was produced by Armstrong's picture of the French robbery, that the attitude in which England was placed by the correspondence between P. & Wellesly was overlooked. The public attention is beginning to fix itself on the proof it affords that the original sin agst. Neutrals lies with G. B. & that whilst she acknowledges it, she persists in it.

I am preparing for a departure from this place immediately after the 4th. July. Having been deprived of the Spring visit to My Farm, I wish to commence the sooner the fall recess. Be assured of my highest & most affe. esteem.

[P.S.] Have you recd. a Copy of Coopers (the Pena. Judge) masterly opinion on the question whether the sentence of a foreign admiralty court in a prize Cause, be conclusive evidence in a suit here between the Underwriter & Insured. It is a most *thorough* investigation, and irreparable disproof of the B. Doctrine on the subject, as adopted by a decision of the Supreme Court of the U. S.? If you are without a copy I will provide & forward one.

†From: Madison Papers, Library of Congress.

# 11

# Napoleon Reacts to Macon's Bill No. 2, 1810

As Madison had noted to the American minister in London, there was a chance that Napoleon would decide "to turn the tables on G. Britain by compelling her either to revoke her orders, or to lose the commerce of this Country" (Madison to Pinkney, May 23, 1810). John Armstrong, the American minister in Paris, sent Napoleon's foreign secretary a copy of a newspaper that contained Macon's Bill No. 2. In this unusual way the bait offered by Congress to either France or England attracted Napoleon's attention. The Duke of Cadore may have had reservations, but Napoleon did not, and on Agust 5, 1810, the American minister received an official note from the French government informing him that the Berlin and Milan decrees would be canceled on November 1 provided either the Orders in Council of 1807 were revoked or that Congress and the President would implement section four of the Macon's Bill No. 2 (and deny all further commerce between the United States and England). On the face of things, the French statement (known to history as the Duke of Cadore's letter) was a kind of "put up or shut up" proposition *provided* Napoleon sincerely entered into the arrangement. Experience was to prove otherwise, but meanwhile the bait tossed to France was now coming back to the Americans and Madison, for whatever reasons (but mainly because he thought France the least offensive of the two belligerents), grabbed the hook himself. Thereafter, the diplomacy of the day revolved around the subtle question: were the French decrees revoked or were they only cancelled on a piece of paper? The British said they wanted real evidence of a French revocation before they would act, and the French protested that they were acting in good faith. So Madison had to decide whether to call Napoleon a liar, which would throw the United States into England's arms, or pretend that Napoleon was an honorable man. Between the choice of a Frenchman's lie or a British crown of thorns, Madison decided to dissemble. If a French dictator could be bold, so could a president of the United States!

In such circumstances, Lord Wellesley was ill-fitted to serve as an Anglo-American conciliator. When Pinkney received a letter from Armstrong giving an account of the Duke of Cadore's letter, Pinkney in effect turned to the British and said, "Now, in the light of what Napoleon has done, will you finally admit the Orders in Council were wrong and revoke them?" Wellesley simply spoke for the nation when he said—what is your proof that the French have revoked their decrees? What Wellesley was unable to perceive was a tendency on the part of Americans to believe the worst about England and the best about France (the New England Federalists excepted, for with them, it was the other way around). "That the American government and people were infected with a deadly hatred toward England, if not already true, was becoming true with a rapidity which warranted Wellesley in taking it for fact, if he could do nothing to prevent it. . . . In truth his colleagues had as little reason to expect war with America as he had to charge the American government with 'deadly affection' toward France" (Adams, *History*, vol. 5, p. 273). A definite blind spot existed in the British cabinet meetings, and perhaps in the American ones as well; but at least in the British meetings they could point to a string of successes (impressment, Orders in Council, Rule of 1756, the *Chesapeake* affair) and they were fairly smug in their belief that American patience was limitless. They forgot that 1812 was an election year. Madison put his ear to the ground and decided the nation was losing patience.

### Document 11-a†

## The Duke of Cadore to General Armstrong

(translation)

SIR:                                                              PARIS, *August* 5, 1810.

I have laid before His Majesty, the Emperor and King, the act of Congress of the 1st of May, taken from the Gazette of the United States, which you have sent to me.

His Majesty could have wished that this act, and all the other acts of the Government of the United States, which interest France, had always been officially made known to him. In general, he has only a knowledge of them indirectly, and after a long interval of time. There have resulted from this delay serious inconveniences, which would not have existed if these acts had been promptly and officially communicated.

The Emperor had applauded the general embargo laid by the United States on all their vessels, because that measure, if it has been prejudicial to France, had in it at least nothing offensive to her honor. It has caused her to lose her colonies of Martinique, Guadaloupe, and Cayenne; the Emperor has not complained of it. He has made this sacrifice to the principle which had determined the Americans to lay the embargo, inspiring them with the noble resolution of interdicting to themselves the ocean, rather than to submit to the laws of those who wished to make themselves the tyrants (*les dominateurs*) of it.

The act of the 1st March has raised the embargo, and substituted for it a measure the most injurious to the interests of France.

This act, of which the Emperor knew nothing until very lately, interdicted to American vessels the commerce of France, at the time it authorized that to Spain, Naples, and Holland, that is to say, to the countries under French

†From: *American State Papers: Foreign Relations*, vol. 3, pp. 386-87.

influence, and denounced confiscation against all French vessels which should enter the ports of America. Reprisal was a right, and commanded by the dignity of France, a circumstance on which it was impossible to make a compromise (*de transiger*.) The sequestration of all the American vessels in France has been the necessary conquence of the measure taken by Congress.

Now Congress retrace their steps, (*revient sur ses pas;*) they revoke the act of the 1st of March; the ports of America are open to French commerce, and France is no longer interdicted to the Americans; in short, Congress engages to oppose itself to that one of the belligerent Powers which should refuse to acknowledge the rights of neutrals.

In this new state of things, I am authorized to declare to you, sir, that the decrees of Berlin and Milan are revoked, and that after the 1st of November they will cease to have effect; it being inderstood that, in conseouence of this declaration, the English shall revoke their orders in council and renounce the new principles of blockade, which they have wished to establish; or that the United States, conformably to the act you have just communicated, shall cause their rights to be respected by the English.

It is with the most particular satisfaction, sir, that I make known to you this determination of the Emperor. His Majesty loves the Americans. Their prosperity and their commerce are within the scope of his policy.

The independence of America is one of the principal titles of glory to France. Since that epoch, the Emperor is pleased in aggrandizing the United States, and, under all circumstances, that which can contribute to the independence, to the prosperity, and the liberty of the Americans, the Emperor will consider as conformable with the interests of his empire. Accept, sir, the assurance of my high consideration

### Document 11-b†

## Madison to Caesar Rodney

Montpellier Sepr 30. 1810

Dear Sir

I am just favored with yours of the 26th. & sincerely sympathize with you in the loss you have sustained.

The new scene opened by the revocation of the Fr. Decrees, will I hope, terminate in a removal of the embarrassments which have been as afflicting as they have been unexampled. It promises us at least an extrication from the dilemma. of a mortifying peace, or a war with both the great belligerents. The precise course which G. B. will take remains to be seen. Whatever the immediate one may be, it is probable that we shall ultimately be at issue with her, or her fictitious blockades

No official communication of the French Act has yet come to hand; and its precise shape can not be inferred from what has appeared, should the

†From: Thomas and Caesar Rodney Papers Library of Congress

letter to Genl. Armstrong be authentic as it probably is, and accurate in its translation, which it probably may not be. In every view important questions will occur as to the construction of the Act of Congs. & the French revocations, in their mutual bearings on each other. It is an occasion therefore in which your legal counsels will be so particularly desireable, that I flatter myself the restoration of your health will enable you to join us at Washington in time to afford us that advantage. I propose to set out thither on wednesday morning, & expect to be there on Saturday. By that time the other heads of Depts. will probably all be there. The official communications from Genl. A[rmstrong][1] may of course be hourly looked for; and something also from Mr. P. which may be interesting. Should it be impracticable for you to get to Washington, I must ask the favor of you, as the next best assistance, to consider, & let us know your ideas, on the several points which are likely to come into question, in deliberating on the course to be taken by the [executive], and on the form of a proclamation, best adapted to the case. . . .

## Document 11-c†

### Madison to Jefferson

Washington Ocr. 19, 1810

Dear Sir

I have recd. your favor of the 15th. All we know of the step taken by France towards a reconciliation with us, is thro' the English papers sent by Mr. Pinkney, who had not himself recd. any information on the subject from Genl. A. nor held any conversation with the B. Ministry on it, at the date of his last letters. We hope from the step, the advantage at least of having but one contest on our hands at a time. If G. B. repeals her orders, without discontinuing her Mock-blockades, we shall be at issue with her on ground strong in law, in the opinion of the world, and in her own concessions. And I do not believe that Congs. will be disposed, or permitted by the Nation, to a tame submission; the loss so as it would be not only perfidious to the other belligerent, but irreconciliable with an honorable neutrality. . . .

## Document 11-d‡

### Madison's Proclamation Exempting France from All Commercial Restrictions Imposed by Congress

By the President of the United States                    [November 2, 1810]

#### A Proclamation

*Whereas* by the fourth section of the act of Congress passed on the first day

---

[1]Armstrong's silence, when the United States needed confirmation of Napoleon's sincerity, became a moot point. See Adams, *History*, vol. 5, pp. 250-59, and *American State Papers; Foreign Relations*, vol. 3, p. 388.

†From: Madison Papers, Library of Congress.

‡From: Draft in the hand of Caesar Rodney, Madison Papers, Library of Congress.

of May 1810, entitled "An act concerning the commercial intercourse between the United State, & Great Britain & France & their dependencies, & for other purposes," it is provided "That in case either Great Britain or France shall before the third day of March next, so revoke or modify her edicts, as that they shall cease to violate the neutral commerce of the United States, which fact the President of the United States shall declare by proclamation," then, the restrictions imposed by the said act, "shall cease & be discontinued in relation to the nation so revoking or modifying her decrees,"

*And Whereas,* it has been officially made known to this government, that the French decrees of Berlin & Milan were so revoked, & that they would cease to have effect on the first instant

*Now Therefore* I James Madison President of the United States, do hereby proclaim that the decrees aforesaid have been revoked, & that they ceased to have effect on the first instant, & that from the date of these presents, all the restrictions imposed by the aforesaid act, shall cease & be discontinued in relation to France & her dependencies. . . .

## *Document 11-e†*

### Pinkney to Lord Wellesley

MY LORD:          GREAT CUMBERLAND PLACE, NOVEMBER 3, 1810.

In my note of the 25th of August, I had the honor to state to your lordship that I had received, from the minister plenipotentiary of the United States at Paris, a letter, dated the 6th of that month, in which he informed me that he had received from the French Government a written and official notice that it had revoked the decress of Berlin and Milan, and that, after the 1st of November, those decrees would cease to have any effect; and I expressed by confidence that the revocation of the British orders in council of January and November, 1807, and April, 1809, and of all other orders dependent upon, analogous to, or in execution of them, would follow of course.

Your lordship's reply, of the 31st of August, to that note, repeated a declaration of the British minister in America, made, as it appears, to the Government of the United States in February, 1808, of "His Majesty's earnest desire to see the commerce of the world restored to that freedom which is necessary for its prosperity, and his readiness to abandon the system which had been forced upon him, whenever the enemy should retract the principles which had rendered it necessary;" and added an official assurance that, "whenever the repeal of the French decrees should have actually taken effect, and the commerce of the neutral nations should have been restored to the condition in which it stood previously to the promulgation of those

†From: *American State Papers: Foreign Relations,* vol. 3, p. 373.

decrees, His Majesty would feel the highest satisfaction in relinquishing a system which the conduct of the enemy compelled him to adopt."

Without departing in any degree from my first opinion, that the United States had a right to expect, upon every principle of justice, that the prospective revocation of the French decrees would be immediately followed by at least a like revocation of orders of England, I must remind your lordship, that the day has now passed when the repeal of Berlin and Milan edicts, as communicated to your lordship in the note above mentioned, and published to the whole world by the Government of France in the Moniteur of the 9th of September, was, by the terms of it, to take effect. That it has taken effect cannot be doubted, and it can as little be questioned that, according to the repeated pledges given by the British Government on this point, (to say nothing of various other powerful considerations,) the prompt relinquishment of the system to which your lordship's reply to my note of the 25th of August alludes, is indispensable.

I need scarcely mention how important it is to the trade of the United States, that the Government of Great Britain should lose no time in disclosing, with frankness and precision, its intentions on this head. Intelligence of the French repeal has reached America, and commercial expeditions have, doubtless, been founded upon it. It will have been taken for granted that the British obstructions to those expeditions, having thus lost the support, which, however insufficient in itself, was the only one that could ever be claimed for them, have been withdrawn; and that the seas are once more restored to the dominion of law and justice.

I persuade myself that this confidence will be substantially justified by the event, and that to the speedy recall of such orders in council as were subsequent in date to the decrees of France, will be added the annulment of the antecedent order, to which my late letter respecting blockades particularly relates. But if, notwithstanding the circumstances which invite to such a course, the British Government shall have determined not to remove those obstructions with all practicable promptitude, I trust that my Government will be apprized, with as little delay as possible, of a determination so unexpected, and of such vital concern to its rights and interests; and that the reasons upon which that determination may have been formed will not be withheld from it.

I have the honor to be, with high consideration, my lord, your lordship's most obedient, humble servant,

### Document 11-f†

## Jonathan Russell to the Duke of Cadore

Sir                                                            Paris, *December* 10 1810.

I have this moment learned that the American brig, the New Orleans Packet, lately arrived at Bordeaux, has with her cargo, the *bona fide* property of citizens of the United States, and laden at the port of New York, been seized by the director of the customs under the Berlin and Milan decrees. I

†From: *American State Papers*: Foreign Relations, vol. 3, p. 391.

have also been informed that this director of the customs, not satisfied with this hardy violation of the solemn assurances given by your excellency to General Armstrong on the 5th August last, and confirmed by your letter to him of the 7th September, that these decrees were revoked, and would cease to operate from the 1st November, has, without regard to the plighted faith of his Government, announced his intention of selling the provisions which constitute a part of the cargo, under the pretext that they are perishable. The clear and unequivocal manner in which the revocation of the Berlin and Milan decrees was announced by your excellency, forbids me for a moment to suppose that the violent proceedings of this man will be sanctioned by His Majesty the Emperor and King, or that the least delay will allowed in placing the property thus arrested at the free disposition of the rightful owner, whose confidence alone in the good faith with which it becomes nations to perform their engagements has brought him to the place where he is so inhospitably treated.

I am persuaded that your excellency will not, on this occasion, attempt to remind me of the conditions on which the revocation of those decrees was predicated. These conditions were in the alternative, and the performance of either is sufficient to render absolute and perpetual that revocation. It is of no importance that the British orders in council have not been withdrawn, if the United States, in due time, perform the condition which depends alone on them: and what is this condition? Why, to execute an act of Congress against the English, which, to be thus executed, requires the previous revocation of these very decrees. The letter of your excellency of the 5th August appears to have been written with a full knowledge of this requisition of the law, and manifestly with the intention to comply with it, in order that it might be competent for the President of the United States to exercise the contingent power which had been given to him.

It will not be pretended that the decrees have, in fact, been revoked, but that the delay of the United States in performing the condition presented to them authorizes their revival. The case of the New Orleans Packet is the first which has occurred since the 1st of November, to which the Berlin or Milan decrees could be applied; and if they be applied to this case, it will be difficult for France to show one solitary instance of thier having been practically revoked; as to delay on the part of the United States, there has been none. No official information of the letter of your excellency of the 5th August left France for the United States, owing to circumstances which it was not in the power of General Armstrong to control, until the 29th September; and to this moment I have not learned that such official information has been there received. I might, indeed, have learned it, and been able now to have communicated to your excellency the measures on which the President has decided in consequence of it, had not the frigate, the Essex, despatched by him, been put under quarantine, on her arrival at L'Orient, for the want of a bill of health, and the messenger thereby detained since the 4th of this month. I will not undertake to decide whether a bill of health, ought, in courtesy, to be exacted of a frigate of a friendly Power coming in the *winter season* from a place not known to have been lately afflicted with any malignant disease; but surely the delay which this exaction occasions cannot be imputed to a want of due diligence on the part of the American Government.

It is from this view of the subject that I am thoroughly convinced that the application of the Berlin or Milan decree, by the director of the customs at Bordeaux, to the New Orleans Packet, will not be approved by His Majesty, but that prompt and efficient measures will be taken to correct a procedure which, if persisted in, might produce a state of things which it is the obvious interest of both nations to avoid. I pray your excellency to be assured of my most distinguished consideration.

### Document 11-g†

### Madison to Jefferson

Washington Der. 7. 1810

Dear Sir

... We have nothing from abroad, more than has been made public. The latest date from Pinkney is the 3d. of Ocr. The arrival of Novr. will have been some test, postive or negative of the views of England: Her party here seems puzzled more than usual. If they espouse her Blockades, they must sink under the odium. And this course is the more desperate, as it is possible that she may abandon them herself, under the duress of events. ...

### Document 11-h‡

### Madison's Second State of the Union Message to Congress

Washington, December 5, 1810.

Fellow Citizens of the Senate and of the House of Representatives:

The embarrassment which have prevailed in our foreign relations, and so much employed the deliberations of Congress, make it a primary duty in meeting you to communicate whatever may have occurred in that branch of our national affairs.

The act of the last session of Congress concerning the commercial intercourse between the United States and Great Britain and France and their dependencies having invited in a new form a termination of their edicts against our neutral commerce, copies of the act were immediately forwarded to our ministers at London and Paris, with a view that its object might be within the early attention of the French and British governments.

By the communication received through our minister at Paris it appeared that a knowledge of the act by the French Government was followed by a

†From: Madison Papers, Library of Congress.

‡From: Gaillard Hunt, ed., *The Writings of James Madison*, 9 vols. (New York: G. P. Putnam's Sons, 1900-1910), vol. 8, pp. 123-25.

declaration that the Berlin and Milan decrees were revoked, and would cease to have effect on the 1st day of November ensuing. These being the only known edicts of France within the description of the act, and the revocation of them being such that they ceased at that date to violate our neutral commerce, the fact, as prescribed by law, was announced by a proclamation bearing date of 2d day of November.

It would have well accorded with the conciliatory views indicated by this proceeding on the part of France to have extended them to all grounds of just complaint which now remain unadjusted with the United States. It was particularly anticipated that, as a further evidence of just dispositions toward them, restoration would have been immediately made of the property of our citizens seized under a misapplication of the principle of reprisals combined with a misconstruction of a law of the United States. This expectation has not been fulfilled.

From the British Government no communication on the subject of the act has been received. To a communication from our minister at London of a revocation by the French Government of its Berlin and Milan decrees it was answered that the British system would be relinquished as soon as the repeal of the French decrees should have actually taken effect and the commerce of neutral nations have been restored to the condition in which it stood previously to the promulgation of those decrees. This pledge, although it does not necessarily import, does not exclude the intention of relinquishing, along with the orders in council, the practice of those novel blockades which have a like effect of interrupting our neutral commerce, and this further justice to the United State is the rather to be looked for, inasmuch as the blockades in question, being not more contrary to the established law of nations than inconsistent with the rules of blockade formally recognized by Great Britain herself, could have no alleged basis other than the pleas of retaliation alleged as the basis of the orders in council. Under the modification of the original orders of November, 1807, into the orders of April, 1809, there is, indeed, scarcely a nominal distinction between the orders and the blockades. One of those illegitimate blockades, bearing date of May, 1806, having been expressly avowed to be still unrescinded, and to be in effect comprehended in the orders in council, was too distinctly brought within the purview of the act of Congress not to be comprehended in the explanation of the requisites to a compliance with it. The British Government was accordingly apprised by our minister near it that such was the light in which the subject was to be regarded.

On the other important subjects depending between the United States and that Government no progress has been made from which an early and satisfactory result can be relied on.

In this new posture of our relations with those powers the consideration of Congress will be properly turned to a removal of doubts which may occur in the exposition, and of difficulties in the execution, of the act above cited. . . .

# 12

# Poised Between British Indifference and French Callousness, 1811

Madison's annual message to Congress in December, 1810 had been a curious admission that nobody really knew what was going on—and an invitation in these peculiar circumstances was extended to Congress to proceed warily. The news from France was not encouraging at all, and yet Madison's proclamation was now an albatross around the Republican party's neck. The debate over a new charter for the Bank of the United States was almost a relief, and this languishing discussion allowed the nation to forget temporarily the quandary produced by Napoleon's alleged revocation of the Berlin and Milan decrees. John Wayles Eppes, one of Madison's staunchest supporters in the House, brought in new nonintercourse bill. Eppes's bill seemed to admit that something was not quite right about the president's proclamation of the last fall (November 2, 1810) so that the endorsement of Congress to his act was offered; but the legislation was less than forthright. However, the bill passed and therefore sanctioned Madison's declaration of French compliance with Macon's Bill No. 2, while closing the door to further importations of English goods in English ships. Thus the effect of Eppes's bill was to throw American hopes for peace as a kind of lifebuoy to the British, but the Englishmen did not think they were sinking—they thought quite the reverse—and so the expectation that the Orders in Council might be revoked seemed as far away as ever. Grasping at every straw, Madison and his supporters heard that the king was again incapacitated by madness and the Prince Regent was said to be a flexible man who might favor rescinding the detested Orders in Council.

*Document 12-a†*

## Debates in Congress on the Nonintercourse Bill
### Saturday, February 2.

...Mr. Eppes said he had no objection to state the reasons which operated with him [in asking for a recommitting of the nonintercourse bill to the proper committee]. The bill contained various provisions respecting enforcing the law of May last. The non-intercourse went into operation to-day. It had been considered by the Committee of Foreign Relations that, in the present aspect of our affairs, it would be better to provide for the relief of our own citizens, and suspend the passage of the law for enforcing the non-intercourse, until the doubts hanging over our foreign relations were dissipated. Under these impressions, the Committee had though it proper that a distinct bill should be reported, to admit to entry all vessels sailing from Great Britain after the second of February. ... [Mr. Randolph wished to know if he could make a motion amending Eppes's motion to recommit, and was told that this would be in order.] ... The amendment which he wished to propose, Mr. R. said, was one which he should have wished to have offered in the shape of a separate resolution, and which he came down to the House to-day prepared to offer. He should make but few prefatory remarks on the subject. Time was short; was precious; and, above all, he should wish the House to act with promptitude, in whatsoever it might decide on this question.... nothing was farther from his policy, than a desire to create an unpleasant sensation or reflection in the mind of any member of this House—it would be recollected, he said, that we had made a sort of retreat from the embargo to the non-intercourse law. Among the objections which then suggested themselves to the friends as well as the opponents of that law, the ingenious one which has been taken in France never once occurred; it was not contended, he believed, that it would give to that Government a plea for heavy retaliation on us. Such, however, was the fact. The sequestrations and confiscations of American property in France, have been made avowedly in retaliation of the non-intercourse law number one. From that law, however, we escaped to another position, changed our front, and took post on the act (he forgot the title of it) concerning commercial intercourse, &c.—the act of the last session. And now, Mr. R. said, it seemed they were to have a modification of that....

Nothing was further from his wish, Mr. R. said, than to enter into a detailed exposition of our foreign relations, but he asked all sides of the House to lay their hands on their hearts and ask themselves what benefits had accrued from the nonintercourse law No. 1, and that of last session, No. 2? Why did they continue on the statute book those acts? Why were these measures, totally imbecile as relates to foreign Powers, altogether inadequate as to coercion on them, suffered to remain in existence? ...

†From: *Annals of Congress*, 11th Cong., 3d sess, February 2, 1811, pp. 863-68.

All he would wish to press upon the House was, the propriety of relieving the President of the United States from the dilemma in which he must now stand, in conséquence of his proclamation, by an immediate repeal of that law of commercial intercourse to which this new bill from the Committee of Foreign Relations is supplementary. Mr. R., therefore, moved, by way of amendment, that the Committee of Foreign Relations be instructed to bring in a bill to repeal the bill respecting commercial intercourse between the United States and Great Britain and France, and their dependencies. I make this you motion, said Mr. R., and, for God's sake, let us once more have clear stays.

Mr. Eppes said it was . . . sufficient for him to observe that the Executive had complied with the law of last session; that the Berlin and Milan decrees having been withdrawn, and these being the only decrees "violating the neutral commerce of the United States," in consequence of that withdrawal, the President had issued the proclamation required by law. With regard to the injuries received from each belligerent, Mr. E. said, he would not pass through the chapter of wrongs. . . . [There was evidence of some infringements by France since last August, but the circumstances are not fully known, and Eppes would not vote to repeal the old nonintercourse bill unless he saw] unequivocal evidence that France has violated the faith pledged to this nation.

The arrangement with France stands precisely on the same footing as with Great Britain. In both cases the Executive accepted the faith of the nation, pledged through their Minister; and if it should turn out that we have been deceived by both, it will prove that there has been always on the part of the Executive of the United States a sincere disposition to have peace with these nations. . . .

[Mr. Randolph said] . . . With regard to the anxiety of the President to preserve peace, Mr. R. presumed there could be no doubt of the fact; he never doubted it. He submitted to the House whether late occurrences did not afford an opportunity of getting rid of this wretched system of lame expedients, in which they had embarked since they abandoned the embargo. It might be said that in a short time news might be received of the repeal of the Orders in Council, which would, in the opinion of some, render this motion unnecessary. The law, Mr. R. said, was a rule of conduct for him, and no foreign nation had a right to know of its existence; and if news of rescinding the Orders in Council were to arrive in town this day, he should still be clearly of opinion that they ought to repeal this law [Macon's Bill No. 2]. He looked upon the law as being mischievous; as having no operation on the Orders in Council or Bonaparte's decrees. If it had none, why retain it? Why keep it here as a germ of difficulty? Let us have clear stays, I repeat, said Mr. R. Let us have *tabular rasa*; and, if we must fight, let us fight without parchment chains about our hands.

[The debate continued for much of the day until a vote on Randolph's motion to call for repeal of Macon's Bill No. 2 was taken. The motion lost, forty-five to sixty-seven.]

## Document 12-b†

### Eppes's Nonintercourse Supplementary Bill, 1811

A Bill supplementary to the act, entitled "An act concerning the commercial intercourse between the United States and Great Britain and France, and their dependencies, and for other purposes."

*Be it enacted, &c.*, That no vessel, owned wholly be a citizen or citizens of the United States, which shall have departed from a British port, prior to the 2d day of February, 1811, and no merchandise owned wholly by a citizen or citizens of the United States, imported in such vessel, shall be liable to seizure or forfeiture on account of any infraction or presumed infraction of the provisions of the act to which this act is a supplement.

Sec. 2. *And be it further enacted*, That, in case Great Britain shall so revoke or modify her edicts, as that they shall cease to violate the neutral commerce of the United States, the President of the United States shall declare the fact by proclamation; and such proclamation shall be admitted as evidence, and no other evidence shall be admitted of such revocation or modication in any suit or procecution which may be instituted under the fourth section of the act to which this act is a supplement. And the restrictions imposed, or which may be imposed, by virtue of the said act, shall, from the date of such proclamation, cease and be discontinued.

Sec. 3 *And be it further enacted*, That, until the proclamation aforesaid shall have been issued, the several provisions of the third, fourth, fifth, sixth, seventh, eighth, ninth, tenth, and eighteenth sections of the act, entitled "An act to interdict the commercial intercourse between the United States and Great Britain and France and their dependencies, and for other purposes," shall have full force and be immediately carried into effect against Britain, her colonies, and dependencies. . . .

## Document 12-c‡

### Madison to Jefferson

Washington Mar. 18. 1811

Dear Sir

. . . A sketch in manuscript was brought by yesterday's Mail from N. York, saying that a vessel just arrived, stated that the Prince Regent had appointed his Cabinet; that Lord Holland was prime Minister, Grenville Secretary of State, Moira Commander in Chief &c. and that a new Parliament was to be called. Whether these details be correct or not, it is highly probable that some material change in the general policy of the Government, in relation to this Country as well as in other respects, will result from the

---

†From: *Annals of Congress*, 11th Cong., 3d sess, February 28, 1811, pp. 1095-96.
‡From: Madison Papers, Library of Congress.

change of the Men in power. Nor is it improbable that a repeal of the orders in Council, will be accompanied by a removal in some form or other, of the other condition required by the Act of May last. Still the attachment to maritime usurpations on public law, and the jealousy of our growing commerce, are sources from which serious difficulties must continue to flow, unless controuled by the distress of the Nation, or by a magnanimity not to be expected even from the personification of Fox in Lord Holland. Grenville is known to be very high in his notions of British rights on the ocean; but he has never contended for more, on the subject of blockades, than that a cruising squadrons, creating manifest danger in entering particular ports, was equivalent to a stationary force, having the same effect. His principle however tho' construable into an important restriction of that modern practice, may be expanded so as to cover this abuse. It is, as you remark, difficult to understand the meaning of Bonaparte towards us. There is little doubt, that his want of money, and his ignorance of commerce, have had a material influence. He has also distrusted the stability & efficacy of our pledge to renew the non-intercourse agst. G. B. and has wished to execute his in a manner that would keep pace only with the execution of ours; and at the same time leave no interval for the operation of the British orders, without a counter operation in either his or our measures. In all this, his folly is obvious. Distrust on one side produces & authorizes it on the other; and must defeat every arrangement between parties at a distance from each other or which is to have a future or a continued execution. On the whole our prospects are far from being very flattering; yet a better chance seems to exist than, with the exception of the adjustment with Erskine, has presented itself, for closing the scene of rivalship in plundering & insulting us, & turning it into a competition for our commerce & friendship. . . .

# 13

## Monroe Joins the Cabinet, but Nothing Else is Changed, 1811

After a winter so harsh that Jefferson commented on its severity, the spring thaws did nothing for Anglo-American relations. The only noteworthy event of the winter was the political effort to oust Gallatin, which boomeranged. This interfamily fight resulted in Madison's determination to drop the millstone, Robert Smith, from the State Department and replace him with James Monroe. Monroe briefly had flirted with Madison's enemies in 1808 and let them try to start a "Stop Madison" campaign that would have denied the White House to Madison. The movement fizzled, and after a cooling-off period Madison made overtures to Monroe through a mutual friend. On April Fool's Day, 1811, Monroe became secretary of state, and from that time forward there was more guidance and rapport than had existed between the White House and the State Department since Jefferson and Madison had worked together.

The summer of 1811 proved to be one of discontent, however. There was no good news on the official dispatch ships, and after Pinkney quitted London it seemed that official relations between England and America were at their lowest ebb since Washington sent John Jay to London to avert a war in 1794. The congressional elections in 1810 had sent a more vocal band of representatives to Washington, moreover, and when the War Hawks got together in their Capitol Hill boarding houses in 1811 there was no talk of olive branches or doves of peace. The London newspapers reported this bold and bellicose spirit, but the British cabinet was in no hurry to seek a détente with the United States as long as business prospered.

*Document 13-a†*

### Madison to Jefferson

Washington Apl. 1. 1811

Dear Sir

... You will have inferred the change which is taking place in the Dept. of State. Col. Monroe agrees to succeed Mr. Smith, who declines however the

†From: Madison Papers, Library of Congress.

mission to Russia, at first not unfavorably looked at. I was willing, notwithstanding many trying circumstances, to have smoothed the transaction as much as possible, but it will be pretty sure to end in secret hostility, if not open warfare. On account of my great esteem & regard for common friends such a result is truly painful to me. For the rest, ˙ feel myself on firm ground, as well in the public opinion, as in my own consciousness.

... The latest information from Europe will be found in the inclosed papers. The indications from France are rather favorable. Should the Old King displace the Regent in England, little is to be hoped from that quarter; unless forced on the Cabinet by national distress. In the last correspondence of Pinkney with Wellesley, the latter sufficiently showed his teeth and recd. the severest scourging that was ever diplomatically inflected. Be assured always of my great esteem & affection

## Document 13-b†

[Madison received scores of petitions from New England town meetings begging for some relief from restrictions on American shipping. He no doubt would have answered this one from New Haven in the expectation it would be reprinted in the newspapers and thus furnish a general reply.]

### To the Inhabitants of the Town of New Haven

Washington May 24. 1811.

I have recd. fellow Citizens, the petition which you have addressed to me representing the inconveniences experienced from the existing non-importation law, and soliciting that the National Legislature may be speedily convened.

It is known to all that the Commerce of the U. S. has, for a considerable period, been greatly abridged & annoyed by Edicts of the Belligerent powers; each professing retaliation only on the other; but both violating the clearest rights of the U. S. as a neutral nation. In this extraordinary state of things, the Legislature willing to avoid a resort to war, more especially during the concurrent aggressions of two great Powers, themselves at war, the one with the other, and determined on the other hand agst an unqualified acquiescence, have endeavored by successive and varied regulations affecting the commerce of the parties, to make it their interest to be just.

In the Act of Congress out of which the existing non-importation has grown, the state of Commerce was not otherwise qualified than by a provision, that in case either of the Belligerents should revoke its unlawful Edicts, and the other should fail to do the same, our ports should be shut to the vessels & merchandize of the latter. This provision which, like our previous offers, repelled the very pretext set up by each, that its Edicts agst. our trade with the other, was required by our acquiescence in the like Edicts of the other, was equally presented to the attention of both. In consequence of the

†From: Madison Papers, Library of Congress.

communication the French Government declared that its Decrees were revoked. As the British Government had expressed reluctance in issuing its orders, and repeatedly signified a wish to find in the example of its adversary, an occasion for putting an end to them, the expectation was the more confident, that the occasion would be promptly embraced. This was not done; and the period allowed for the purpose having elapsed, our ports became shut to British Ships and merchandize. Whether the conduct of the French Government has been, and will be such as to satisfy the authorized expectations of the U. States; or whether the British Government may have opened, or will open the way for the Executive removal of the restrictions on British commerce with the U. States, which it continues in its power to do, by revoking its own unlawful restrictions on our commerce, is to be ascertained by further information; which will be received & employed by the Executive with that strict impartiality, which has been invariably maintained towards the two Belligerents.

Whatever may be the inconveniences resulting in the mean time, from the non-importation Act, it was not to have been supposed, that whilst it falls within the necessary power, and practice of regulating our commercial intercourse with foreign Countries, according to circumstances, the act would be regarded as not warranted by the Constitution; or that whilst it was a partial restriction only, and had for its object, an entire freedom of our commerce, by a liberation of it from foreign restrictions unlawfully imposed, it could be viewed as destroying commerce; and least of all that a likeness could be seen between a law enacted by the representatives of the Country, with a view to the interest of the Country, and Acts of a Government in which the country was not represented, framed with a view to the interest of another Country, at the expence of this.

If appeals to the justice of the Belligerents, through their interest, involve privations on our part also, it ought to be recollected that this is an effect inseparable from every resort, by which one nation can right itself agst. the injustice of others.

If sacrifices made for the sake of the whole result more to some than to other districts or descriptions of Citizens, this also is an effect, which tho always to be regretted, can never be entirely avoided. Whether the appeal be to the sword, or to interruptions or modifications of customary intercourse, an equal operation on every part of the Community never happen. Nor would an unqualified acquiescence in belligerent restrictions on our commerce, if that could be reconciled with what the nation owes to itself, be less unequal in its effects on different local situations & interests.

In estimating the particular measure which has been adopted by the National Councils, it may be reasonably expected therefore, from the candor of enlightened Citizens, that with the peculiarity of the public situation, they will be impressed also with the difficulty of selecting the course most satisfactory, and best suited to diminish its evils or shorten their duration: that they will keep in mind that a resort to war must involve necessary restrictions on commerce; and that were no measure whatever opposed to the

Belligerent acts against our Commerce, it would not only remain under the severe restrictions now imposed by foreign hands, but new motives would be given for prolonging and invigorating them.

These observations are not meant to anticipate the policy which the legislature may henceforward find best adapted to support the honor or promote the interest of the Nation; or to prejudge questions relative to particular changes which may be pointed out by experience, or be called for by the state of our foreign relations. Neither do they imply any predetermination as to the measure of convening the Legislature, which it will be a duty to adopt or decline as our national affairs may appear to require. The view of our situation presented to your patriotic reflections, has been suggested by that contained in your address; and it will have its desired effect, if it recalls your attention to the peculiar embarrassments with which the national Councils have had to contend, and enforces the importance of manifesting that union of all in supporting the measures of the Constituted authorities whilst actually in force, which is as necessary to their effect at home, and abroad, as it is consistent with the right and with the legitimate modes, of seeking a revisal of them. In the mode which the Town of New Haven has employed I witness with satisfaction, that in exercising the right of freemen, the obligation of Citizens has not been forgotten; and that it affords a pledge and an example which I am far from undervaluing. I tender you my respects and my friendly wishes.

### Document 13-c†

## Madison to Jefferson

Washington July 8. 1811

Dear Sir;

[Robert Smith's pamphlet is being discussed, and "his infamy is daily fixing itself upon him," while Smith vainly tries to throw "his guilt on others"] . . . .
As the latest information from Russel, is prior to the arrival of the non-importation act, the state of our affairs at Paris may be conjectured. Pinkney brings, of course, nothing; Foster being the channel of English news. I do not know that he has yet opened himself compleatly to Mr. Monroe; but from the conciliatory disposition of the Prince Regent, and the contrary one of his Cabinet, still deriving an ascendency from the convalescence of the King, you will be unable to dive into the character of the mission. You will perceive in the printed paper enclosed, a step by the British Minister, which, very unreasonably it would seem, denotes an increasing rigor towards this country, according to a preceding interposition with the Court of admiralty, cases under the orders in Council had been suspended. . . .

†From: Madison Papers, Library of Congress.

*Document 13-d†*

## Monroe to Augustus J. Foster, the British Minister
## to the United States

Sir:                          DEPARTMENT OF STATE, *October* 1, 1811.

I have had the honor to receive your letter of the 26th of July, and to submit it to the view of the President. In answering that letter, it is proper that I should notice a complaint that I had omitted to reply in mine of the 23d of July to your remonstrance against the proclamation of the President of November last, and to the demand which you had made, by the order of your Government, of the repeal of the non-importation act of March 2d of the present year.

My letter has certainly not merited this imputation.

Having shown the injustice of the British Government in issuing the orders in council, on the pretext assigned, and its still greater injustice in adhering to them after that pretext had failed, a respect for Great Britain, as well as for the United States, prevented my placing, in the strong light in which the subject naturally presented itself, the remonstrance alluded to, and the extraordinary demand founded on it, that while your Government accommodated in nothing, the United States should relinquish the ground which, by a just regard to the public rights and honor, they had been compelled to take. Propositions tending to degrade a nation can never be brought into discussion by a Government not prepared to submit to the degradation. It was for this reason that I confined my reply to those passages in your letter, which involved the claim of the United States, on the principles of justice, to the revocation of the orders in council. Your demand, however, was neither unnoticed nor unanswered. In laying before you the complete, and, as was believed, irresistible proof on which the United States expected and called for the revocation of the orders in council, a very explicit answer was supposed to be given to that demand.

Equally unfounded is your complaint, that I misunderstood that passage which claimed, as a condition of the revocation of the orders in council, that the trade of Great Britain with the continent should be restored to the state in which it was before the Berlin and Milan decrees were issued. As this pretension was novel and extraordinary, it was necessary that a distinct idea should be formed of it, and, with that view, I asked such an explanation as would enable me to form one.

In the explanation given, you do not insist on the right to trade, in British property, with British vessels, directly with your enemies. Such a claim, you admit, would be preposterous. But you do insist, by necessary implication, that France has no right to inhibit the importation into her ports of British manufactures, or the produce of the British soil, when the property of neutrals; and that, until France remove that inhibition, the United States are to be cut off by Great Britain from all trade whatever with her enemies.

On such a pretension it is almost impossible to reason. There is, I believe,

†From: *American State Papers: Foreign Relations*, vol.3, pp. 445-56.

no example of it in the history of past wars. Great Britain, the enemy of France, undertakes to regulate the trade of France. Nor is that all; she tells her that she must trade in British goods. If France and Great Britain were at peace, this pretension would not be set up, nor even thought of. Has Great Britain then acquired, in this respect, by war, rights which she has not in peace? And does she announce to neutral nations, that, unless they consent to become the instruments of this policy, their commerce shall be annihilated, their vessels shall be shut up in their own ports?

I might ask whether French goods are admitted into Great Britain, even in peace; and if they are, whether it be of right, or by the consent and policy of the British Government?

That the property would be neutralized does not affect the question. If the United States have no right of carry their own productions into France without the consent of the French Government, how can they undertake to carry there those of Great Britain? In all cases it must depend on the interest and the will of the party.

Nor is it material to what extent, or by what powers, the trade to the continent is prohibited. If the Powers who prohibit it are at war with Great Britain, the prohibition is a necessary consequence of that state. If at peace, it is their own act; and whether it be voluntary or compulsive, they alone are answerable for it. If the act be taken at the instigation and under the influence of France, the most that can be said is, that it justifies reprisal against them by a similar measure. On no principle whatever can it be said to give any sanction to the conduct of Great Britain towards neutral nations.

The United States can have no objection to the employment of their commercial capital in the supply of France, and of the continent generally, with manufactures, and to comprise in the supply those of Great Britain, provided those Powers will consent to it. But they cannot undertake to force such supplies on France, or on any other Power, in compliance with the claim of the British Government, on principles incompatible with the rights of every independent nation; and they will not demand in favor of another Power what they cannot claim for themselves.

All that Great Britain could with reason complain of was, the inhibition, by the French decrees, of the lawful trade of neutrals with the British dominions. As soon as that inhibition ceased, her inhibition of our trade with France ought, in like manner, to have ceased. Having pledged herself to proceed *pari passu* with France, in the revocation of their respective acts, violating neutral rights, it has afforded just cause of complaint, and even of astonishment, to the United States, that the British Government should have sanctioned the seizure and condemnation of American vessels, under the orders in council, after the revocation of French decrees was announced, and even in the very moment when your mission, avowed to be conciliatory, was to have its effect. I will only add, that had it appeared, finally, that France had failed to perform her engagement, it might at least have been expected that Great Britain would not have molested such of the vessels of the United States as might be entering the ports of France, on the faith of both Governments, until that failure was clearly proved.

To many insinuations in your letter I make no reply, because they sufficiently suggest the only one that would be proper.

If it were necessary to dwell on the impartiality which has been observed by the United States towards the two belligerents, I might ask, whether, if Great Britain had accepted the condition which was offered equally to her and France, by the act of May 1st, 1810, and France had rejected it, there is cause to doubt that the non-importation act would have been carried into effect against France? No such doubt can possibly exist, because, in a former instance, when the Government, trusting to a fulfilment by yours of an arrangement which put an end to a non-intercourse with Great Britain, the non-intercourse was continued against France, who had not then repealed her decrees, as it was not doubted that England had done. Has it not been repeatedly declared to your Government, that if Great Britain would revoke her orders in council, the President would immediately cause the non-importation act to cease? You well know that the same declaration has been often made to yourself, and that nothing is wanting to the removal of the existing obstructions to the commerce between the two countries, than a satisfactory assurance, which will be received with pleasure from yourself, that the orders in council are at an end.

By the remark in your letter of the 3d of July, that the blockade of May, 1806, had been included in the more comprehensive system of the orders in council of the following year, and that, if that blockade should be continued in force after the repeal of the orders in council, it would be in consequence of the special application of a sufficient naval force, I could not but infer your idea to be, that the repeal of the orders in council would necessarily involve the repeal of the blockade of May. I was the more readily induced to make this inference, from the consideration, that, if the blockade was not revoked by the repeal of the orders in council, there would be no necessity for giving notice that it would be continued, as by the further consideration, that, according to the decison of your Court of Admiralty, a blockade instituted by proclamation does not cease by the removal of the force applied to it, not without a formal notice by the Government to that effect.

It is not, however, wished to discuss any question relative to the mode by which that blockade may be terminated. Its actual termination is the material object for consideration.

It is easy to show, and it has already been abundantly shown, that the blockade of May, 1806, is inconsistent, in any view that may be taken of it, with the law of nations. It is also easy to show that, as now expounded, it is equally inconsistent with the sense of your Government when the order was issued; and this change is a sufficient reply to the remarks which you have applied to me personally. . . .

The United States have not, nor can they approve the blockade of an extensive coast. Nothing, certainly, can be inferred from any thing that has passed relative to the blockade of May, 1806, to countenance such an inference.

It is seen with satisfaction that you still admit that the application of an adequate force is necessary to give a blockade a legal character, and that it will lose that character whenever that adequate force ceases to be applied. As it cannot be alleged that the application of any such adequate force has been continued, and actually exists, in the case of the blockade of May, 1806, it would seem to be a fair inference that the repeal of the orders in council will leave no insuperable difficulty with respect to it. To suppose the contrary would be to suppose that the orders in council, said to include that blockade, resting themselves on a principle of retaliation only, and not sustained by the application of an adequate force, would have the effect of sustaining a blockade admitted to require the application of an adequate force, until such adequate force should actually take the place of the orders in council. Whenever any blockade is instituted, it will be a subject for consideration; and if the blockade be in conformity to the law of nations, there will be no disposition in this Government to contest it.

I have the honor to be, &c.

## Document 13-e†

### Madison's State of the Union Message

Washington November 5th 1811

Fellow Citizens of the Senate, and of the House of Representatives.

In calling you together sooner than a separation from your homes, would otherwise have been required,[1] I yielded to considerations, drawn from the posture of our foreign affairs; and in fixing the present, for the time of your meeting; regard was had to the probability of further developements of the policy of the Belligerent Powers towards this Country, which might the more unite the national councils, in the measures to be pursued.

At the close of the last session of Congress, it was hoped, that the successive confirmations of the extinction of the French Decrees, so far as they violated our neutral commerce, would have induced the Government of Great Britain to repeal its orders in council; and thereby authorize a removal of the existing obstructions, to her commerce with the United States.

Instead of this reasonable step towards satisfaction and friendship between the two nations, the orders were, at a moment when least to have been expected, put into more rigorous execution; and it was communicatied through the British Envoy just arrived, that, whilst the revocation of the Edicts of France, as officially made known to the British Government, was denied to have taken place; it was an indispensable condition of the repeal of the British orders, that commerce should be restored to a footing, that would admit the productions and manufactures of Great Britain, when owned by neutrals, into markets shut against them by her Enemy: the United States being given to understand that, in the mean time, a continuance of their non-importation Act, would lead to measures of retaliation.

---

†From:  Records of the House of Representatives, National Archives.

[1]Madison called a special session of Congress so that the lawmakers could convene a month early.

At a later date, it has indeed appeared, that a communication to the British Government, of fresh evidence of the repeal of the French Decrees against our neutral trade, was followed by an intimation, that it had been transmitted to the British Plenipotentiary here; in order that it might receive full consideration, in the depending discussions. This communication appears not to have been received: But the transmission of it hither, instead of founding on it, an actual repeal of the orders, or assurances that the repeal would ensue, will not permit us to rely, on any effective change in the British cabinet. To be ready to meet with cordiality, satisfactory proofs of such a change; and to proceed, in the mean time, in adopting our measures to the views which have been disclosed through that Minister, will best consult our whole duty.

In the unfriendly spirit of those disclosures, indemnity and redress for other wrongs, have continued to be withheld; and our coasts and the mouths of our harbours, have again witnessed scenes, not less derogatory to the dearest of our national rights, than vexations to the regular course of our trade.

Among the occurrences produced by the conduct of British ships of war, hovering on our Coasts, was an encounter between one of them, and the American Frigate commanded by Captain Rodgers, rendered unavoidable on the part of the latter, by a fire, commenced without cause, by the former; whose commander is, therefore, alone chargeable with the blood unfortunately shed, in maintaining the honor of the American flag. The proceedings of a Court of Enquiry requested by Captain Rodgers, are communicated together with the correspondence relating to the occurrence between the Secretary of State and His Britannic Majesty's Envoy. To these are added, the several correspondences, which have passed on the subject of the British Orders in Council; and to both, the correspondence relating to the Floridas, in which Congress will be made acquainted with the interposition, which the Government of Great Britain, has thought proper to make, against the proceedings of the United States.

The justice and fairness which have been evinced on the part of the United States towards France, both before and since the revocation of her Decrees, authorized an expectation, that her Government would have followed up that measure, by all such others as were due to our reasonable claims, as well as dictated by its amicable professions. No proof, however, is yet given, of an intention to repair the other wrongs done to the United States; and particularly, to restore the great amount of American property, seized and condemned, under Edicts; which, though not affecting our neutral relations, and therefore not entering into questions between the United States and other Belligerents, were nevertheless founded in such unjust principles, that the reparation ought to have been prompt and ample.

In addition to this, and other demands of strict right, on that nation: the United States have much reason to be dissatisfied with the rigorous and unexpected restrictions on importations from France into the United States. . . .

I must now add, that the period is arrived, which claims from the Legislative Guardians of the National rights, a system of more ample provisions for maintaining them. Notwithstanding the scrupulous justice, the protracted moderation, and the multiplied efforts on the part of the United States, to substitute, for the accumulating dangers to the peace of the two Countries, all the mutual advantages of re-established friendship and confidence; we have seen that the British Cabinet perseveres, not only in withholding a remedy for other wrongs, so long and and so loudly calling for it; but in the execution, brought home to the threshold of our Territory, of measures which, under existing circumstances, have the character, as well as the effect, of war on our lawful commerce.

With this evidence of hostile inflexibility in trampling on rights which no Independent Nation can relinquish; Congress will feel the duty of putting the United States into an armour, and an attitude demanded by the crisis, and corresponding with the national spirit and expectations.

I recommend, accordingly, that adequate provision be made, for filling the ranks, and prolonging the enlistments of the regular troops; for an auxiliary force, to be engaged for a more limited term; for the acceptance of volunteer corps, whose patriotic ardor may court a participation in urgent services; for detachments, as they be wanted, of other portions of the militia; and for such a preparation of the great Body, as will proportion its usefulness, to its intrinsic capacities. Nor can the occasion fail to remind you, of the importance of those Military Seminaries, which, in every event, will form a valuable and frugal part of our Military establishment. . . .

In contemplating the scenes which distinguish this momentous Epoch, and estimating their claims to our attention, it is impossible to overlook those developing themselves, among the great communities, which occupy the southern portion of our own hemisphere, and extend into our neighbourhood. An enlarged philanthropy, and an enlightened forecast, concur in imposing on the National Councils, an obligation to take a deep interest in their destinies; to cherish reciprocal sentiments of good will; to regard the progress of Events; and not to be unprepared, for whatever order of things, may be ultimately established.

Under another aspect of our situation, the early attention of Congress will be due, to the expediency of further guards, against evasions and infractions of our Commercial laws. The practice of smuggling, which is odious every where, and particularly criminal in free Governments, where, the laws being made by all for the good of all, a fraud is committed on every individual as well as on the State, attains its utmost guilt, when it blends with a pursuit of ignominious gain, a treacherous subserviency, in the transgressions, to a foreign policy, adverse to that of their own Country. It is then, that the virtuous indignation of the public, should be enabled to manifest itself, through the regular animadversions, of the most competent laws. . . .

The receipts into the Treasury, during the year ending on the thirtieth of September last, have exceeded thirteen Millions and a half of Dollars; and have enabled us to defray the current expenses, including the Interest on the public debt, and to reimburse more than five Millions of Dollars, of the principal; without recurring to the loan authorized by the Act of the last session. The temporary loan obtained in the latter end of the year one thousand eight hundred and ten, has also been reimbursed, and is not included in that amount.

The decrease of revenue arising from the situation of our commerce, and the extraordinary expences which have and may become necessary, must be taken into view, in making commensurate provisions for the ensuing year. And I recommend to your consideration, the propriety of ensuring a sufficiency of annual revenue, at least to defray the ordinary expences of Government, and to pay the interest on the public debt; including that on the new loans which may be authorized.

I cannot close this communication, without expressing my deep sense of the crisis in which you are assembled, my confidence in a wise and honorable result to your deliberations, and assurances of the faithful zeal with which my co-operating duties will be discharged; invoking, at the same time, the blessing of Heaven on our beloved Country, and on all the means that may be employed, in vindicating its rights, and advancing its welfare.

# 14

# Tippecanoe, John Henry, and the Hornet Comes Home Empty-Handed

When news reached the seaboard of the short but bloody battle in the Indiana Territory at Tippecanoe, Americans were quick to assert that the Indians had been urged to their challenge of Governor Harrison's troops by British agents. Newspapers teemed with war talk as the ardent Republicans vowed that the impressment of seamen, the harassment of American commerce all over the globe, and now the blood-curdling yell of the drunken Indian—all were sufficient provocation for war. The British minister in Washington wanted to make it clear that his country had nothing to do with frontier warfare, but the image of red-coated savages taking their cue from Canadian bases was fixed in the westerners' minds. The House of Representatives prepared for war by issuing a committee report (the "Porter Report" see Document 14-a) that was a full catalog of American grievances, intended to prove that America had borne with patience a series of British acts that no sovereign nation could continue to ignore. There was almost a hint of an ultimatum in the congressional manifesto, and Madison hoped it would alarm the British leaders into realizing that this was the eleventh hour—that after nearly seven years a decision for war was at hand unless Britain revoked the Orders in Council and sent that happy news on the *Hornet*, a dispatch ship that was to bring home news either of peace or of war.

While awaiting the arrival of the *Hornet*, Madison and Monroe became dupes for a smooth-talking Frenchman, who promised to deliver incriminating evidence that would rock Federalist Boston to its Beacon Hill foundations. The president and his secretary of state recoiled at the asking price—$75,000—for this useful information. Finally, $50,000 of public funds was paid for the Henry letters, and a bad bargain it turned out to be. The letters were no more revealing than the columns of Benjamin Russell's *Columbian Centinel*, and after much bluster in Congress the incident (and bad investment in war scares) counted for little.

What did make an impression was the arrival in May of the long-awaited

*Hornet.* The news was disappointing—England was going ahead with her orders. France was not keeping her end of the bargain struck by the Duke of Cadore's letter, but between the two belligerents there was no doubt in Madison's mind that one stood foremost as the stumbling block to America's nationhood. If it was old-fashioned to talk of "the chains of slavery" fashioned by George III's minions, so be it. James Madison was an old-fashioned Republican who loved his country too much to allow further insults and embarrassments to sap the strength of the Union

## Document 14-a†

### The War Hawks Send Their Report
REPORTED TO CONGRESS, NOVEMBER 29 1811.

The committee to whom was referred that part of the President's message which relates to our foreign affairs, beg. leave to report, in part:

That they have endeavored to give to the subject submitted to them that full and dispassionate consideration which is due to one so intimately connected with the interest, the peace, the safety, and the honor of their country.

Your committee will not encumber your journals and waste your patience with a detailed history of all the various matters growing out of our foreign relations. The cold recital of wrongs, of injuries and aggressions known and felt by every member of this Union, could have no other effect than to deaden the national sensibility, and render the public mind callous to injuries with which it is already too familiar.

Without recurring, then, to the multiplied wrongs of partial or temporary operation, of which we have so just cause of complaint against the two great belligerents, your committee will only call your attention at this time to the systematic aggressions of those Powers, authorized by their edicts against neutral commerce—a system which, as regarded its principles, was founded on pretensions that went to the subversion of our national independence; and which, although now abandoned by one Power is, in its broad and destructive operation as still enforced by the other, sapping the foundations of our prosperity.

It is more than five years since England and France, in violation of those principles of justice and public law, held sacred by all civilized nations, commenced this unprecedented system, by seizing the property of the citizens of the United States, peaceably pursuing their lawful commerce on the high seas. To shield themselves from the odium which such outrage must incur, each of the belligerents sought a pretext in the conduct of the other—each attempting to justify his system of rapine, as a retaliation for similar acts on the part of his enemy. As if the law of nations, founded on the eternal rules of justice, could sanction a principle, which, if engrafted into our municipal code, would excuse the crime of *one* robber, upon the sole plea

†From: *American State Papers: Foreign Relations*, vol. 3, pp. 537-38

that the unfortunate object of his rapacity was also a victim to the injustice of another. The fact of priority could be true as to one only of the parties; and, whether true or false, could furnish no ground of justification.

The United States thus unexpectedly and violently assailed by the two greatest Powers in Europe, withdrew their citizens and property from the ocean; and, cherishing the blessings of peace, although the occasion would have fully justified war, sought redress in an appeal to the justice and magnanimity of the belligerents. When this appeal had failed of the success which was due to its moderation, other measures, founded on the same pacific policy, but applying to the interests instead of the justice of the belligerents, were resorted to. Such was the character of the non-intercourse and non-importation laws, which invited the return of both Powers to their former state of amicable relations, by offering commercial advantages to the one who should first revoke his hostile edicts, and imposing restrictions on the other.

France, at length, availing herself of the proffers made equally to her and her enemy by the non-importation law of May, 1810, announced the repeal, on the 1st of the following November, of the decrees of Berlin and Milan. And it affords a subject of sincere congratulation to be informed, through the official organs of the Government, that those decrees are, so far at least as our rights are concerned, really and practically at an end.

It was confidently expected that this act on the part of France would have been immediately followed by a revocation on the part of Great Britain of her orders in council. If our reliance on her justice had been impaired by the wrongs she had inflicted, yet, when she had plighted her faith to the world that the sole motive of her agressions on neutral commerce was to be found in the Berlin and Milan decrees, we looked forward to the extinction of those decrees as the period when the freedom of the seas would be again restored.

In this reasonable expectation we have, however, been disappointed. A year has elapsed since the French decrees were rescinded, and yet Great Britain, instead of retracing *pari passu* that course of unjustifiable attack on neutral rights, in which she professed to be only the reluctant follower of France, has advanced with bolder and continually increasing strides. To the categorical demands lately made by our Government for the repeal of her orders in council, she has affected to deny the practical extinction of the French decrees; and she has, moreover, advanced a new and unexpected demand, increasing in hostility the orders themselves. She has insisted, through her accredited minister at this place, that the repeal of the orders in council must be preceded, not only by the practical abandonment of the decrees of Berlin and Milan, so far as they infringe the neutral rights of the United States, but by the renunciation, on the part of France, of the whole of her system of commercial warfare against Great Britain, of which those decrees originally formed a part.

This system is understood to consist in a course of measures adopted by France, and the other Powers on the continent subject to or in alliance with her, calculated to prevent the introduction into their territories of the products and manufactures of Great Britain and her colonies, and to annihilate her trade with them. However hostile these regulations may be on the part of France towards Great Britain, or however sensibly the latter may feel their effects, they are, nevertheless, to be regarded only as the expedients of one enemy against another, for which the United States, as a neutral Power, can in no respect be responsible; they are, too, in exact conformity with those which Great Britain has herself adopted and acted upon, in time of peace as well as war. And it is not to be presumed that France would yield to the unauthorized demand of America what she seems to have considered as one of the most powerful engines of her present war.

Such are the pretensions upon which Great Britain founds the violation of the maritime rights of the Unites States—pretensions not theoretical merely, but followed up by a desolating war upon our unprotected commerce. The ships of the United States, laden with the products of our own soil and labor, navigated by our own citizens, and peaceably pursuing a lawful trade, are seized on our own coasts, at the very mouths of our harbors, and condemned and confiscated.

Your committee are not, however, of that sect whose worship is at the shrine of a calculating avarice. And while we are laying before you the just complaints of our merchants against the plunder of their ships and cargoes, we cannot refrain from presenting to the justice and humanity of our country the unhappy case of our impressed seamen. Although the groans of these victims of barbarity for the loss of (what should be dearer to Americans than life) their liberty—although the cries of their wives and children in the privation of protectors and parents have, of late, been drowned in the louder clamors at the loss of property; yet is the practice of forcing our mariners into the British navy, in violation of the rights of our flag, carried on with unabated rigor and severity. If it be our duty to encourage the fair and legitimate commerce of this country by protecting the property of the merchant, then, indeed, by as much as life and liberty are more estimable than ships and goods, so much more impressive is the duty to shield the persons of our seamen, whose hard and honest services are employed, equally with those of the merchants, in advancing, under the mantle of its laws, the interests of their country.

To sum up, in a word, the great causes of complaint against Great Britain, your committee need only say, that the United States, as a sovereign and independent Power, claim the right to use the ocean, which is the common and acknowledged highway of nations, for the purposes of transporting, in their own vessels, the products of their own soil, and the acquisitions of their own industry, to a market in the ports of friendly nations; and to bring home, in return, such articles as their necessities or convenience may require; always regarding the rights of belligerents, as defined by the established law of nations. Great Britain, in defiance of this incontestable right, captures every American vessel bound to, or returning from, a port where her commerce is not favored, enslaves our seamen, and, in spite of our remonstrances, perseveres in these aggressions.

To wrongs so daring in character, and so disgraceful in their execution, it is impossible that the people of the United States should remain indifferent. We must now tamely and quietly submit, or we must resist by those means which God has placed within our reach.

Your committee would not cast a shade over the American name, by the expression of a doubt which branch of this alternative will be embraced. The occasion is now presented when the national character, misunderstood and traduced for a time by foreign and domestic enemies, should be vindicated.

If we have not rushed to the field of battle like the nations who are led by the mad ambition of a single chief, or the avarice of a corrupted court, it has not proceeded from a fear of war, but from our love of justice and humanity. That proud spirit of liberty and independence, which sustained our fathers in the successful assertion of their rights against foreign aggression, is not yet sunk. The patriotic fire of the revolution still burns in the American breast with a holy and unextinguishable flame, and will conduct this nation to those high destinies, which are not less the reward of dignified moderation than of exalted valor.

But we have borne with injury until forbearance has ceased to be a virtue. The sovereignty and independence of these States, purchased and sanctified by the blood of our fathers, from whom we received them, not for ourselves only, but as the inheritance of our posterity, are deliberately and systematically violated. And the period has arrived when, in the opinion of your committee, it is the sacred duty of Congress to call forth the patriotism and resources of the country. By the aid of these, and with the blessing of God, we confidently trust we shall be enabled to procure that redress which has been sought for by justice, by remonstrance, and forbearance, in vain.

Your committee, reserving for a future report of those ulterior measures which, in their opinion, ought to be pursued, would, at this time, earnestly recommend, in the words of the President, "That the United States be immediately put into an armor and attitude demanded by the crisis, and corresponding with the national spirit and expectations." And, to this end, they beg leave to submit, for the adoption of the House, the following resolutions:

1. *Resolved*, That the military establishment, as authorized by existing laws, ought to be immediately completed, by filling up the ranks and prolonging the enlistments of the troops; and that, to encourage enlistments, a bounty in lands ought to be given, in addition to the pay and bounty now allowed by law.

2., That an additional force of ten thousand regular troops ought to be immediately raised, to serve for three years; and that a bounty in lands ought to be given to encourage enlistments.

3. That it is expedient to authorize the President, under proper regulations, to accept the service of any number of volunteers, not exceeding fifty thousand, to be organized, trained, and held in readiness to act on such service as the exigencies of the Government may require.

4. That the President be authorized to order out, from time to time, such detachments of the militia as, in his opinion, the public service may require.

5. That all the vessels not now in service, belonging to the navy and

worthy of repair, be immediately fitted up and put in commission.

6. That it is expedient to permit our merchant vessels, owned exclusively by resident citizens, and commanded and navigated solely by citizens, to arm, under proper regulations to be prescribed by law, in self-defence, against all unlawful proceedings against them on the high seas.

## Document 14-b†

### Augustus J. Foster to Monroe

Sir:                                                      Washington, *December* 28, 1811.

I have been informed by Mr. Morier that, so long ago as the 1st of last January, in consequence of a written communication from Sir James Craig, His Majesty's Governor General, and Commander-in-chief in Canada, dated the 25th November, 1810, acquainting him with his suspicions of its being the intention of some of the Indian tribes, from the great fermentation among them, to make an attack on the United States, and authorizing him to impart his suspicions to the American Secretary of State, he had actually done so verbally to Mr. Smith, your predecessor in office, and on searching among the archives of this mission, I have found the letter alluded to of Sir James Craig, by which he did authorize Mr. Morier to make the communication in question, as well as a memorandum of its having so been made; as also an express declaration of Sir James Craig, that, although he doubted there would not be wanting persons who whould be ready to attribute the movements of the Indians to the influence of the British Government, yet, that his department were actually making every exertion in their power to assist in preventing their attempts.

This evidence, sir, of a friendly disposition to put the United States' Government on their guard against the machinations of the savages, and even to aid in preventing the calamity which has taken place, is so honorable to the Governor General of Canada, and so clearly in contradiction to the late unfounded reports which have been spread of a contrary nature, that I cannot resist the impulse I have to draw your attention towards it; not that I conceive, however, that it was necessary to produce this proof to the United States' Government of the falsity of such reports, which the character of the British nation, and the manifest inutility of urging the Indians to their destruction, should have rendered improbable, but in order that you may be enabled, in case it shall seem fitting to you, by giving publicity to this letter, to correct the mistaken notions on the subject, which have unfortunately found their way even among persons of the highest respectability, only, as I am convinced, from their having been misinformed. I have the honor to be, with the highest consideration, sir, Your most obedient, humble servant,

†From: *American State Papers: Foreign Relations*, vol. 3, p. 453.

*Document 14-c†*

## John Henry's Overture to Monroe, 1812

Sir:                                     PHILADELPHIA, *February* 20, 1812.

Much observation and experience have convinced me, that the injuries and insults with which the United States have been so long and so frequently visited, and which cause their present embarrassment, have been owing to an opinion entertained by foreign States, "*that in any measure tending to wound their pride, or provoke their hostility, the Government of this country could never induce a great majority of its citizens to concur.*" And as many of the evils which flow from the influence of this opinion on the policy of foreign nations may be removed by any act that can produce *unanimity among all parties in America*, I voluntarily tender to you, sir, such means as I possess towards promoting so desirable and so important an object; which, if accomplished, cannot fail to extinguish, perhaps forever, those expectations abroad, which may protract indefinitely an accommodation of existing differences, and check the progress of industry and prosperity in this rising empire.

I have the honor to transmit, herewith, the documents and correspondence relating to an important mission, in which I was employed by Sir James Craig, the late Governor General of the British provinces in North America, in the winter of the year 1809.

The publication of these papers will demonstrate a fact, not less valuable than the good already proposed; it will prove that no reliance ought to be place on the professions of good faith of an administration which, by a series of disastrous events, has *fallen* into such hands as a Castlereagh, a Wellesley, or a Liverpool. I should rather say into the hands of the stupid subalterns, to whom the pleasures and the indolence of those ministers have consigned it.

In contributing to the good of the United States, by an exposition which cannot, I think, fail to solve and melt all division and disunion among its citizens, I flatter myself with the fond expectation that, when it is made public in England, it will add one great motive to the many that already exist, to induce that nation to withdraw its confidence from *men, whose political career is a fruitful source of injury and embarrassment in America: of injustice and misery in Ireland; of distress and apprehension in England; and contempt every where.*

In making this communication to you, sir, I deem it incumbent upon me distinctly and unequivocally to state that I adopt no party views; that I have not changed any of my political opinions; that I neither seek nor deserve the patronage nor countenance of any Government, nor of any party; and that, in addition to the motives already expressed, *I am influenced by a just resentment of the perfidy and dishonor of those who first violated the*

---

†From: *American State Papers: Foreign Relations*, vol. 3, p. 545-6.

*conditions upon which I received their confidence:* who have injured me and disappointed the expectations of my friends; and left me no choice but between a degrading acquiescence in injustice and a retaliation which is necessary to secure to me my own respect.

This wound will be felt where it is merited, and if *Sir James Craig* still live, his share of the pain will excite no sympathy among those who are at all in the secret of our connexion. I have the honor to be, sir, your most obedient servant, &c.

## Document 14-d†

### Madison to Joel Barlow[1]

Washington Feby. 24. 1812

Dear Sir

...I see with pleasure the auspicious attentions which have distinguished your intercourse with the F Govt. and the convincing views presented on your part, of the commercial policy which it ought to adopt towards the U.S. From these sources encouragement is drawn. In other respects the prospect suggests distrust rather than expectation. The delay in answering your note, the vagueness of the answer when given; the refusal to sign the contents of the paper presented by you, even in the ordinary & unexceptionable form proposed, and the substitution of a verbal for a written notification of the orders to the Custom Houses &c &c by which our merchants were to be invited to the F. Market, are circumstances which necessarily attract serious notice. The reserve manifested on the subject of the paper alluded to is the more remarkable as a written sanction to it would have so little committed them. Beyond a freedom of the French ports to the products of the U. S. under all the existing limitations & incumbrances, it pledged nothing more than a melioration of formalities as to ownership and origin; leaving Colonial produce on the old footing of special licences. The liberation of the remaining ships & Cargoes could surely created no difficulty, if any real purpose of friendship or good faith be entertained. It would seem therefore that the objection must have lain against the clause forbidding captures & seizures, for other cause than forged papers. The recent condemnations in the Baltic cases, and the avowal of the F. Consul in Denmark that all vessels, *withersoever* bound, with Colonial produce were within the orders to capture, favor this conjecture; and if it be the true one, adjustment is hopeless; and the consequences obvious. I do not forget that your understanding of all these particulars was better than mine can be, and that my constructions may be merely colorable. I wish this may be the case, but we find so little of explicit dealing with substantial redress mingled with the compliments and

---

†From: Madison Papers, Library of Congress.

[1] The American minister in Paris. He was appointed in February 1811 but did not sail for France until July.

encouragements which cost nothing because they may mean nothing, that suspicions are unavoidable; and if they be erroneous, the fault does not lie with those who entertain them.

From the scanty attention I can now give to the subject of a commercial Treaty with F. I am at a loss for the necessity of it, or the motives of F. to set it on foot, if it be not meant to gain time, and be guided by events, on our side we have nothing to stipulate, which is not secured to her, as long as she merits it, by our general system which leaves our exports & imports free, and without any duties on the former, and with moderate ones on the latter. It is on her side that changes & securities are necessary to a friendly reciprocity; and these will for the present be satisfactory to us in the form of stable regulations fairly executed. Among them a reduced tarif favoring *all* our great Staples, and a transit thro' F. ports to inland markets are indispensible to a continued admission of F. Staples. The system of licences must be abolished, if not by F. by us. The neglect of the subject by Cong. is remarkable; but the event cannot be doubtful. Such a mode of commerce corrupts one class of Citizens, and disgusts all the rest; & when the trade licensed is in foreign, not native articles, the evil preponderates still more over the profit. The F. Govt. seems to have taken up a radical error with regard to the commercial interests of the two Countries. It overrates our desire of her commodities. The present footing of the commerce is intolerable to the U. S. and it will be prohibited, if no essential change takes place. . . .

As the Hornet had reached F. before the sailing of the Constitution, and the latter had not a very short passage, we shall soon look for further communications from you. I hope they will correspond equally with your patriotic exertions, and the public calculations. If they do not exhibit the conduct of the F. Govt. in better colors than it has yet assumed, there will be but one sentiment in this country, & I need not say what that will be. Be assured of my affectionate esteem.

### Document 14-e†

## Madison Sends the John Henry Letters to Congress, 1812

MARCH 9, 1812

*To the Senate and House of Representatives of the United States:*

I lay before Congress copies of certain documents, which remain in the Department of State. They prove that, at a recent period, whilst the United States, notwithstanding the wrongs sustained by them, ceased not to observe the laws of peace and neutrality towards Great Britain; and in the midst of amicable professions and negotiations on the part of the British Government, through its public minister here, a secret agent of that Government was employed in certain States, more especially at the seat of Government in

†From: *American State Papers: Foreign Relations,*, vol. 3, p. 545.

Massachusetts, in fomenting disaffection to the constituted authorities of the nation; and in intrigues with the disaffected, for the purpose of bringing about resistance to the laws, and, eventually, in concert with a British force, of destroying the Union and forming the eastern part thereof into a political connexion with Great Britain.

In additon to the effect which the discovery of such a procedure ought to have on the public councils, it will not fail to render more dear to the hearts of all good citizens, that happy union of these States which, under divine Providence, is the guarantee of their liberties, their safety, their tranquillity, and their prosperity.

JAMES MADISON.

MARCH 12, 1812.

*To the Senate of the United States:*
I transmit to the Senate a report of the Secretary of State, complying with their resolution of the 10th instant.*

JAMES MADISON.

## Document 14-f†

### Madison to Jefferson

Dear Sir                                             [March 9, 1812]
As the Intelligencer will not publish the Message & documents just laid before Congs. for the present Mail. I send you a copy of the former. It is justified by the Documents, among which are the original credential & instructions from the Govr. of Canada, and an original dispatch from the Earl of Liverpool to him approving the conduct of the Secret agent. This discovery, or rather formal proof of the cooperation between the Eastern Junto, & the B. Cabinet will, it is to be hoped, not only prevent future evils from that source, but exhort good out of the past.

---

*This resolution was adopted on the motion of Mr. Lloyd, as follows:
*Resolved,* That the Secretary of State be directed to lay before the Senate the names of any and all persons in the United States, and especially in the State of Massachusetts, who have in any way or manner whatever entered into, or most remotely countenanced, the project or the views, for the execution or attainment of which John Henry was, in the year 1809, employed by Sir James Craig, then Governor General of the British provinces in North America, and which have, this day, been communicated to the Senate of the United States.
†From: Madison Papers, Library of Congress.

*Document 14-g†*

## John G. Jackson to Madison

Blacksburg 30th. March 1812

My dear Sir,

It excites the most gloomy reflections that nothing can conquer the inveterate hostility of the opposition: the damning proofs of british perfidy furnished by the documents you communicated to Congress have failed to unite them with the friends of our Country; & the spirit they display in the animadversions with which the presses devoted to them daily teem; as well as in private circles, proves that Great Britain with much justice counts upon a party amongst us. War alone can furnish a remedy for this deplorable malady of the body politic, & a chastisement for insufferable insults daily heaped upon us by the enemy. My voice is for war—& I could willingly add my arm too if we engage in it vigorously. I incline to think (tho' not without some strong suspicions) that the Congress are seriously resolved on war, and as that idea prevails I find the spirit of our young men excited. Tho' I must say that it is a source of surprise to many & of deep regret to me—that notwithstanding some of the most respectable in this quarter were applicants for offices every one of whom we have heard that have succeeded are rank Federalists. You know my friend that I do not, cannot, for a moment listen to the voice of complaint much less cherish it—such things however here, have a bad effect, because in no quarter is the struggle for supremacy between the parties more arduous, or the opposition more malignant. . . .

*Document 14-h‡*

## Madison to Jefferson

Washington April 3. 1812

Dear Sir

. . . A late arrival from G. B. brings dates subsequent to the maturity of the Prince Regents Authority. It appears that Percival, &c. are to retain their places, and that they prefer war with us, to a repeal of their orders in Council. We have nothing left therefore, but to make ready for it. As a step to it an embargo for 60 days was recommended to Congs. on wednesday and agreed to in the H. of Rep. by about 70 to 40. The Bill was before the Senate yesterday, who adjourned about 4 or 5 O Clock without a decision. Whether this result was produced by the rule which arms a single member with a veto agst. a decision in one day on a bill, or foretells a rejection of the Bill I have not yet heard. The temper of that body is known to be equivocal. Such a measure, even for a limited and short time, is always liable to adverse as well as favorable consideration; and its operation at this moment, will add fuel to

†From: Madison Papers, Library of Congress.
‡From: Madison Papers, Library of Congress.

party discontent, and interested clamor. But it is a rational & provident measure, and will be relished by a greater portion of the Nation, than an omission of it. If it could have been taken sooner and for a period of 3 or 4 months, it might have inlisted an alarm of the B. Cabinet, for their Peninsular System, on the side of Concessions to us; and wd. have shaken their obstinacy, if to be shaken at all; the successes on that Theatre, being evidently their hold on the P. Regt: and the hold of both on the vanity &, prejudices of the nation. Whether if adopted for 60 days, it may beget apprehensions of a protraction, & thence lead to admissible overtures, before the sword is stained with blood, cannot be foreknown with certainty. Such an effect is not to be counted upon. You will observe, that Liverpool was Secy. for the Foreign Dept. ad interim, & that Castlereagh is the definitive successor of Wellesley. The resignation of this last, who has recd. no other appt is a little mysterious. There is some reason for believing that he is a variance with Percival; or that he distrusts the stability of the existing Cabinet, and courts an alliance with the Grenville party, as likely to overset it. If none of that party desert their colours, the calculation cannot be a very bad one; especially in case of war with the U. S: in addition to the distress of B. trade & manufactures, and the inflammation in Ireland: to any nothing of possible reverses in Spain & Portugal, which alone would cut up the Percival ascendency by the roots. From France we hear nothing. The delay of the Hornet is inexplicable, but on the reproachful supposition, that the F Govt. is waiting for the final turn of things at London, before it takes its course, which justice alone ought to prescribe, towards us. If this be found to be its game, it will impair the value of concessions if made, and give to her refusal of them, consequences it may little dream of. Be assured of my constant and sincerest attachment. . . .

I understand the Embargo will pass the Senate to day, and possibly with an extension of the period to 75, or 90 days.

## Document 14-i†

### The Leading Republican Newspaper Calls for War

[April 14, 1812]

The public attention has been drawn to the approaching arrival of the *Hornet*, as a period when the measures of our government would take a decisive character, or rather their final cast. We are among those who have attached to this event a high degree of importance, and have therefore looked to it with the utmost solicitude.

But if the reports which we now hear are true, that with England all hope of honorable accommodation is at an end, and that with France our negotiations are in a forwardness encouraging expectations of a favorable result, where is the motive for longer delay? The final step ought to be taken,

†From: Washington *National Intelligencer*, April 14, 1812.

and that step is WAR. By what course of measures we have reached the present crisis, is not now a question for patriots and freemen to discuss. It exists: and it is by open and manly war only that we can get through it with honor and advantage to the country. Our wrongs have been great; our cause is just; and if we are decided and firm, success is inevitable.

Let war therefore be forthwith proclaimed against England. With her there can be no motive for delay. Any further discussion, any new attempt at negotiation, would be as fruitless as it would be dishonorable. With France we shall be at liberty to pursue the course which circumstances may require. The advance she has already made by a repeal of her decrees; the manner of its reception by the government, and the prospect which exists of an amicable accommodation, entitle her to this preference. If she acquits herself to the just claims of the United States, we shall have good cause to applaud our conduct in it, and if she fails we shall always be in time to place her on the ground of her adversary. . . .

[There is some apprehension among citizens that America is not prepared and that the United States might be invaded. However, the British army is occupied all over the world.] Can anyone believe that, under such circumstances, the British government could be so infatuated as to send troops here for the purpose of invasion? The experience and the fortune of our Revolution, when we were comparatively in an infant state, have doubtless taught her a useful lesson that she cannot have forgotten. Since that period our populations has increased threefold, whilst hers has remained almost stationary. . . . Have we cause to dread an attack from her neighboring provinces? That apprehension is still more groundless. Seven or eight millions of people have nothing to dread from 300,000. From the moment that war is declared, the British colonies will be put on the defensive, and soon after we get in motion [they] must sink under the pressure.

## Document 14-j†

### James Maury to Madison

[Maury was an old friend of Madison's family who moved from Spotsylvania County, Virginia, to become a commercial agent in Liverpool. He was also the American consul there.]

Liverpool 20 April 1812

Dear Sir,

. . . I wish there was a better prospect than now presents for amicable adjustment between our country & this. It daily appears more & more the determination of administration to continue the orders in council; yet petitions for their revocation increase; as do the prices of Grain & other articles of food, which, adding to the distresses of Manufacturers, has occasioned serious riots in many parts of this Country. Good Wheat is worth 20/ per 70 lb. & expected to be higher. . . .

†From: Madison Papers, Library of Congress.

*Document 14-k†*

## Madison to Jefferson

Washington May 25. 1812

Dear Sir

The inclosed letters came under cover to me, by the Hornet. France has done nothing towards adjusting our differences with her. It is understood that the B[erlin] & M[ilan] Decrees are not in force agst. the U. S. and no contravention of them can be established agst. her. On the contrary positive cases rebut the allegation. Still the manner of the F. Govt. betrays the design of leaving G. B. a pretext for enforcing her O. in C. And in all other respects the grounds of our complaints remain the same. The utmost address has been played off on Mr. Barlow's wishes & hopes; inasmuch that at the Departure of the Hornet which had been so long detained for a final answer, without its being obtained, he looked to the return of the Wasp which had just arrived, without despair of making her the Bearer of some satisfactory arrangement. Our calculations differ widely. In the mean time, the business is become more than ever puzzling. To go to war with Engd. and not with France arms the federalists with new matter, and divides the Republicans some of whom with the Quids make a display of impartiality. To go to war agst. both, presents a thousand difficulties; above all that of shutting all the ports of the Continent of Europe agst. our Cruisers who can do little without the use of them. It is pretty certain also, that it would not gain over the Federalists, who wd. turn all those difficulties agst. the Administration. The only consideration of weight in favor of this triangular war as it is called, is that it might hasten thro' a peace with G. B. or F: a termination, for a while at least, of the obstinate questions now depending with both. But even this advantage is not certain. For a prolongation of such a war might be viewed by both Belligts. as desireable, with as little reason for the opinion, as has prevailed in the past conduct of both. Affectionate respects

†From: Madison Paper, Library of Congress.

# 15

# A Second War for Independence Must be Fought, 1812

There is an old saying—"the things we talk about never happen." Perhaps this is a solace to chronic worriers, but we can discern with little effort that from 1808 onward there was much talk in the United States of a war with England, and yet it happened. Clearly more rapid communications would have helped matters, but the evidence shows that the men closest to the situation in London and in Washington were given many signs of a revocation of the Orders in Council and yet did not see this occur. Only one valid conclusion seems to be offered—that the Madison administration had decided after the Erskine negotiations were repudiated that no real accommodation would ever be offered by the British. Madison never set this fixed idea down on paper, but his actions and those of the American diplomats tend to confirm this judgment. In his war message to Congress, Madison alluded to the Erskine negotiations by noting that when the British minister in Washinton sent the tentative agreement home, "A foundation appeared to be laid for a sincere and lasting reconciliation." The harsh reaction of Canning to the Erskine documents, indeed, nudged America toward war at a snail's pace. By June, 1812, Madison had finally decided that all further negotiations were fruitless and damaging to American pride. Americans might not fight for their unsold cotton, or their dry-rotted ships, or their sons in English and French dungeons—but Americans could lump all these things together under the rubric of what they would fight for—national honor. The Republican dilemma, caused by the conflict between political theories and the realities of a world at war, had been solved by a most un-Republican decision to grasp the sword.

*Document†*

Madison's War Message to Congress, 1812

[June 1, 1812]

To the Senate and House of Representatives of the United States.

I communicate to Congress certain Documents, being a continuation of

†From: Hunt, ed., *Writings of Madison* vol. 8, pp. 192-200. Letter owned by Mr. and Mrs. Philip D. Sang, Chicago, Il., 1961.

those heretofore laid before them, on the subject of our Affairs with Great Britain.

Without going back beyond the renewal in 1803, of the war in which Great Britain is engaged, and omitting unrepaired wrongs of inferior magnitude; the conduct of her Government presents a series of acts, hostile to the United States, as an Independent and neutral nation.

British cruisers have been in the continued practice of violating the American flag on the great high way of nations, and of seizing and carrying off persons sailing under it; not in the exercise of a Belligerent right founded on the Law of Nations against an Enemy; but of a municipal prerogative over British subjects. British jurisdiction is thus extended to neutral vessels in a situation where no laws can operate but the law of nations, and the laws of the Country to which the vessels belong; and a self-redress is assumed, which, if British subjects were wrongfully detained and alone concerned, is that substitution of force, for a resort to the responsible sovereign, which falls within the definition of War. Could the seizure of British subjects, in such cases, be regarded as within the exercise of a Belligerent right, the acknowledged laws of war, which forbid an article of captured property to be adjudged, without a regular investigation before a competent Tribunal, would imperiously demand the fairest trial, where the sacred rights of persons were at issue. In place of such a trial, these rights are subjected to the will of every petty commander.

The practice, hence, is so far from affecting British subjects alone, that under the pretext of searching for these, thousands of American Citizens, under the safeguard of public law, and of their national flag, have been torn from their country, and from every thing dear to them; have been dragged on board ships of war of a foreign nation; and exposed, under the severities of their discipline, to be exiled to the most distant and deadly climes, to risk their lives in the battles of their oppressors, and to be the melancholy instruments of taking away those of their own brethren.

Against this crying enormity, which Great Britain would be so prompt to avenge if committed against herself, the United States have, in vain, exhausted remonstrances and expostulations: And that no proof might be wanting of their conciliatory dispositions, and no pretext left for a continuance of the practice, the British Government was formally assured of the readiness of the United States to enter into arrangements, such as could not be rejected, if the recovery of British subjects were real and sole object. The communication passed without effect.

British cruisers have been in the practice also of violating the rights and the peace of our Coasts. They hover over and harass our entering and departing commerce. To the most insulting pretentions, they have added the most lawless proceedings in our very harbors; and have wantonly spilt American blood, within the sanctuary of our territorial jurisdiction. The principles and rules enforced by that nation when a neutral nation, against armed vessels of Belligerents hovering near her coasts, and disturbing her commerce, are well known. When called on, nevertheless, by the United States to punish the greater offences committed by her own vessels, her Government has bestowed on their commanders, additional marks of honor and confidence.

Under pretended blockades, without the presence of an adequate force, and sometimes without the practicability of applying one, our commerce has been plundered in every Sea; the great staples of our Country have been cut off, from their legitimate markets; and a destructive blow aimed at our agricultural and maritime interests. In aggravation of these predatory measures, they have been considered as in force, from the dates of their notification; a retrospective effect being thus added, as has been done in other important cases, to the unlawfulness of the course pursued. And to render the outrage the more signal, these mock blockades, have been reiterated and enforced, in the face of official communications from the British Government declaring, as the true definition of a legal Blockade "that particular ports must be actually invested, and previous warning given to vessels bound to them, not to enter."

Not content with these occasional expedients for laying waste our neutral trade, the cabinet of Great Britain resorted, at length, to the sweeping system of Blockades, under the name of orders in council; which has been moulded and managed, as might best suit its political views, its commercial jealousies, or the avidity of British cruisers.

To our remonstrances against the complicated and transcendent injustice of this innovation, the first reply was that the orders were reluctantly adopted by Great Britain, as a necessary retaliation on decrees of her Enemy proclaiming a general Blockade of the British Isles, at a time when the naval force of that Enemy dared not to issue from his own ports. She was reminded, without effect, that her own prior blockades, unsupported by an adequate naval force actually applied and continued, were a bar to this plea: that executed Edicts against millions of our property, could not be retaliation on Edicts, confessedly impossible to be executed: that retaliation to be just, should fall on the party setting the guilty example, not on an innocent party, which was not even chargeable with an acquiescence in it.

When deprived of this flimsy veil for a prohibition of our trade with her enemy, by the repeal of his prohibition of our trade with Great Britain; her Cabinet, instead of a corresponding repeal, or a practical discontinuance, of its orders, formally avowed a determination to persist in them against the United States, until the markets of her enemy should be laid open to British products: thus asserting an obligation on a neutral power to require one Belligerent to encourage, by its internal regulations, the trade of another Belligerent; contradicting her own practice towards all nations, in peace as well as in war; and betraying the insincerity of those professions, which inculcated a belief that having resorted to her orders with regret, she was anxious to find an occasion for putting an end to them.

Abandoning still more all respect for the neutral rights of the United States, and for its own consistency, the British Government now demands, as prerequisites to a repeal of its orders, as they relate to the United States, that a formality should be observed in the repeal of the French Decrees nowise necessary to their termination, nor exemplified by British usage; and that the French repeal, besides including that portion of the Decrees which operate within a territorial jurisdiction, as well as that which operates on the high seas against the commerce of the United States, should not be a single and special repeal in relation to the United States, but should be extended to whatever other neutral nations, unconnected with them, may be affected by those Decrees. And as an additional insult, they are called on for a formal disavowal 'of conditions and pretentions advanced by the French Government, for which the United States are so far from having made themselves responsible; that in official explanations, which have been published to the world, and in a correspondence of the American Minister at London with the British Minister for foreign affairs, such a responsibility was explicitly and emphatically disclaimed.

It has become indeed sufficiently certain, that the commerce of the United States is to be sacrificed, not as interfering with the Belligerent rights of Great Britain; not as supplying the wants of her enemies, which she herself supplies; but as interfering with the monopoly which she covets for her own commerce and navigation. She carries on a war against the lawful commerce of a friend, that she may the better carry on a commerce with an enemy; a commerce polluted by the forgeries and perjuries, which are, for the most part, the only passports by which it can succeed.

Anxious to make every experiment, short of the last resort of injured nations, the United States have withheld from Great Britain, under successive modifications, the benefits of a free intercourse with their market; the loss of which could not but outweigh the profits accruing from her restrictions of our commerce with other nations. And to entitle these experiments to the more favorable consideration, they were so framed, as to enable her to place her adversary under the exclusive operation of them. To these appeals her Government has been equally inflexible; as if willing to make sacrifices of every sort, rather than yield to the claims of justice, or renounce the errors of a false pride. Nay, so far were the attempts carried, to overcome the attachment of the British Cabinet to its unjust Edicts, that it received every encouragement within the competency of the Executive branch of our Government, to expect that a repeal of them would be followed by a war between the United States and France, unless the French Edicts should also be repealed. Even this communication, although silencing for ever the plea of a disposition in the United States to acquiesce in those Edicts, originally the sole plea for them, received no attention.

If no other proof existed of a predetermination of the British Government against a repeal of its orders, it might be found in the correspondence of the Minister Plenipotentiary of the United States at London and the British Secretary for Foreign Affairs, in 1810, on the question whether the Blockade of May 1806 was considered as in force, or as not in force. It had been ascertained that the French Government, which urged this Blockade as the ground of its Berlin Decree, was willing, in the event of its removal, to repeal that Decree; which being followed by alternate repeals of the other offensive

Edicts, might abolish the whole system on both sides. This inviting opportunity for accomplishing an object so important to the United States, and professed so often to be the desire of both the Belligerents, was made known to the British Government. As that Government admits that an actual application of an adequate force is necessary to the existence of a legal Blockade, and it was notorious, that if such a force had ever been applied, its long discontinuance had annulled the Blockade in question, there could be no sufficient objection on the part of Great Britain to a formal revocation of it; and no imaginable objection to a declaration of the fact, that the Blockade did not exist. The declaration would have been consistent with the avowed principles of Blockade; and would have enabled the United States to demand from France the pledged repeal of her Decree; either with sucess, in which case the way would have been opened for a general repeal of the Belligerent Edicts; or without success, in which case the United States would have been justified in turning their measures exclusively against France. The British Government would, however, neither rescind the Blockade, nor declare its non-existence; nor permit its non-existence to be inferred and affirmed by the American Plenipotentiary. On the contrary by representing the Blockade to be comprehended in the orders in Council, the United States were compelled so to regard it, in their subsequent proceedings.

There was a period when a favorable change in the policy of the British Cabinet, was justly considered as established. The Minister Plenipotentiary of His Britannic Majesty here proposed an adjustment of the differences more immediately endangering the harmony of the two Countries. The proposition was accepted with the promptitude and cordiality corresponding with the invariable professions of this Government. A foundation appeared to be laid for a sincere and lasting reconciliation. The prospect, however, quickly vanished. The whole proceeding was disavowed by the British Government, without any explanation which could, at that time, repress the belief, that the disavowal proceeded from a spirit of hostility to the commercial rights and prosperity of the United States. And it has since come into proof, that at the very moment, when the public Minister was holding the language of friendship, and inspiring confidence in the sincerity of the negociation with which he was charged, a secret agent of his Government was employed in intrigues, having for their object, a subversion of our Government, and a dismemberment of our happy union.

In reviewing the conduct of Great Britain towards the United States, our attention is necessarily drawn to the warfare just renewed by the Savages, on one of our extensive frontiers; a warfare which is known to spare neither age nor sex, and to be distinguished by features peculiarly shocking to humanity. It is difficult to account for the activity, and combinations, which have for some time been developing themselves among tribes in constant intercourse with British traders and garrisons, without connecting their hostility with that influence; and without recollecting the authenticated examples of such interpositions, heretofore furnished by the officers and agents of that Government.

Such is the spectacle of injuries and indignities which have been heaped on our Country: and such the crisis which its unexampled forbearance and conciliatory efforts have not been able to avert. It might at least have been expected, that an enlightened nation, if less urged by moral obligations, or invited by friendly dispositions on the part of the United States would have found, in its true interest alone, a sufficient motive to respect their rights and their tranquility on the high seas; that an enlarged policy would have favored that free and general circulation of commerce, in which the British nation is at all times interested, and which in times of war, is the best alleviation of its calamities to herself, as well as to other Belligerents; and, more especially, that the British Cabinet, would not, for the sake of a precarious and surreptitious intercourse with hostile markets, have persevered in a course of measures, which necessarily put at hazard the invaluable market of a great and growing Country, disposed to cultivate the mutual advantages of an active commerce.

Other Councils have prevailed. Our moderation and conciliation, have had no other effect than to encourage perseverance, and to enlarge pretentions. We behold our Seafaring Citizens still daily victims of lawless violence committed on the great common and high way of nations, even within sight of the Country which owes them protection. We behold our vessels, freighted with the products of our soil and industry, or returning with the honest proceeds of them, wrested from their lawful destinations, confiscated by prize Courts, no longer the organs of public law, but the instruments of arbitrary Edicts; and their unfortunate crews dispersed and lost, or forced, or inveigled in British ports, into British fleets: whilst arguments are employed, in support of these aggressions, which have no foundation but in a principle equally supporting a claim, to regulate our external commerce, in all cases whatsoever.

We behold, in fine, on the side of Great Britain a state of War against the United States; and on the side of the United States, a state of peace towards Great Britain.

Whether the United States shall continue passive under these progressive usurpations, and these accumulating wrongs; or, opposing force to force in defence of their national rights, shall commit a just cause into the hands of the almighty disposer of events; avoiding all connections which might entangle it in the contests or views of other powers, and preserving a constant readiness to concur in an honorable re-establishment of peace and friendship, is a solemn question, which the Constitution wisely confides to the Legislative Department of the Government. In recom_nending it to their early deliberations, I am happy in the assurance, that the decision will be worthy the enlightened and patriotic councils, of a virtuous, a free and a powerful Nation.

Having presented this view of the relations of the United States with Great Britain, and of the solemn alternative growing out of them, I proceed to remark, that the communications last made to Congress, on the subject of our relations with France will have shown, that since the revocation of her

Decrees, as they violated the neutral rights of the United States, her Government has authorized illegal captures, by its privateers and public ships: and that other outrages have been practiced, on our vessels and our citizens. It will have been seen also, that no indemnity had been provided or satisfactorily pledged, for the extensive spoliations committed under the violent and retrospective orders of the French Government, against the property of our Citizens seized wihin the jurisdiction of France. I abstain, at this time, from recommending to the consideration of Congress, definitive measures with respect to that nation, in the expectation, that the result of unclosed discussions between our Minister Plenipotentiary of Paris and the French Government, will speedily enable Congress to decide, with greater advantage, on the course due to the rights, the interests, and the honor of our Country. [Congress heard the message with mixed feelings and no sense of urgency. A declaration of war was not passed until June 18, when the British minister was handed his passports and informed that a state of war existed between the United States and Great Britain.]

# Part three

# Bibliographic Essay

Except for some denigrating suggestions between 1968 and 1972 that there were great similarities between the unpopularity of the War of 1812 and the Vietnam campaigns, there has been a marked decline in concern for "Mr. Madison's War" in recent years. Wars are of perpetual interest, of course, so that the relative paucity of material on the war of 1812 may only indicate that it is still an unpopular war, but still (as this book is meant to show) there is reason to contemplate its origins and meaning in the whole conception of American nationhood. This idea is brought forth in Henry Steele Commager's excellent short essay in the June 17, 1962 issue of the *New York Times Magazine*. Walter Lord's *The Dawn's Early Light* (New York, 1972) and John K. Mahon's *The War of 1812* (Gainesville, Fla., 1972) are recent and readable accounts of the military and naval action. Mahon's bibliography is fairly exhaustive, and taken with similar listings in the Perkins and Coles books (cited below) only a tiny paragraph will have escaped the determined student seeking information on writings pertinent to this all-too-neglected phase of American history.

## Suggestions for Further Reading

### Books

Henry Adams, *The History of the United States.* ... 9 vols. (New York, 1962 reprint). History in the grand old manner, full of prejudices but also vivaciously told from the best sources of Adams's time (the 1880s).

Roger H. Brown, *The Republic in Peril: 1812* (New York, 1964). Emphasis in the early chapters is on the difficulties confronting the Republican philosophers-turned-presidents. The footnotes are somewhat unique.

Alfred L. Burt, *The United States, Great Britain and British North America...* (New York, 1961 reprint). Now somewhat superceded by Perkins' work, this valuable book still is important for its insights and reliance on manuscript sources not seen by Adams.

Harry L. Coles, *The War of 1812* (Chicago, 1965). The best summary account of the war and its preliminary diplomacy.

Reginald Horsman, *The Causes of the War of 1812* (Philadelphia, 1962). Stresses the role of Canada in the thinking of War Hawks, and has an exhaustive bibliography.

Bradford Perkins, *Prologue to War: England and the United States 1805-1812* (Berkeley, 1961). Highly readable and soundly researched volume which clarifies the diplomacy of the period.

Julius W. Pratt, *The Expansionists of 1812* (New York, 1925). A pioneer work with interesting but overstated thesis on the role played by the westerners in bringing on war.

James F. Zimmerman, *The Impressment of American Seamen* (New York, 1925). Still the standard treatment on this vexing problem.

### Articles

Warren H. Goodman, "The Origins of the War of 1812: A Survey of Changing Interpretations," *Mississippi Valley Historical Review* 27 (1941); 171-86.

Margaret K. Latimer, "South Carolina—A Protagonist of the War of 1812," *American Historical Review* 61 (1955-1956); 914-29.

Reginald Horsman, "Western War Aims, 1811-1812," *Indiana Magazine of History* 53 (1957); 1-16.

Abott Smith, "Mr. Madison's War," *Political Science Quarterly* 57 (1942); 229-46.

George R. Taylor, "Agrarian Discontent in the Mississippi Valley Preceding the War of 1812," *Journal of Political Economy* 39 (1931); 486-505.


## General Works

Irving Brant, *James Madison . . .* , 6 vols. (Indianapolis, 1941-1961). The best biographical treatment of Madison's life, although a tendency to gloss over Madison's faults weakens the overall value of the work.

Ralph Ketcham, *James Madison* (New York, 1971). A full account of Madison's life which follows the general outlines of Brant's theme, but includes some documentary evidence that was not available for the larger work.

Dumas Malone, *Jefferson the President Second Term 1805-1809* (Boston, 1974). Particularly able interpretation of the Jefferson-Madison effort to steer a neutral course according to prevailing Republican theories.

# WHITMAN COLLEGE LIBRARY

## DATE DUE

| | | | |
|---|---|---|---|
| | | | |
| | | | |
| | | | |
| | | | |
| | | | |
| | | | |
| | | | |
| | | | |
| | | | |
| | | | |
| | | | |
| | | | |
| | | | |
| | | | |
| | | | |
| | | | |
| | | | |
| | | | |
| GAYLORD | | | PRINTED IN U.S.A. |